ANSWER

the ANSWER

R. A. Torrey

Whitaker House

THE ANSWER

ISBN: 0-88368-539-6
Printed in the United States of America
Copyright © 1999 by Whitaker House

Whitaker House
30 Hunt Valley Circle
New Kensington, PA 15068

Library of Congress Cataloging-in-Publication Data

Torrey, R. A. (Reuben Archer), 1856–1928.
    The answer / by R. A. Torrey.
        p.   cm.
    Includes bibliographical references.
    ISBN 0-88368-539-6 (pbk.)
    1. Theology, Doctrinal Popular works.   I. Title.
  BT77.T67   1999
  230—dc21   99-39489

1 2 3 4 5 6 7 8 9 10 11 12 13 /11 10 09 08 07 06 05 04 03 02 01 00 99

Contents

One

Why Did
Jesus Die?

Why Did Jesus Die?

Without shedding of blood there is no remission.
—Hebrews 9:22

One of the most fundamental, central, and vital doctrines of the Christian faith is the doctrine of the Atonement. Without the biblical doctrine of the Atonement, there is no real Christianity—you have only the Devil's substitute. Without the biblical doctrine of the Atonement, you have no real Gospel but, instead, an entirely false and soul-destroying philosophy.

In the past, I have said, "If a person holds right views about the person of Jesus Christ, he will sooner or later get right views on every other question. But if he holds wrong views about the person of Jesus Christ, he is pretty sure to go wrong on everything else, sooner or later." The same thing can be said about the doctrine of the Atonement. If a person holds right views about the atonement made by Jesus Christ on Calvary's cross, he will sooner or later get right views on every other question. But if he holds wrong views about the Atonement, he is pretty sure to go wrong on everything else, sooner or later.

In this day, we are in great need of teaching on the Atonement—teaching that is definite, clear, accurate, exact, and complete. Not only in Unitarian and Christian Science circles*, but also in circles that are nominally Bible-based—in outwardly Christian colleges, seminaries, pulpits, Sunday school classes, magazines, pamphlets, and books—there is much teaching that is vague, inaccurate, misleading, unscriptural, and often absolutely false and devilish. Much of so-called Christian teaching is essentially the same as that of Unitarianism or Christian Science. Men and women use the old words—such as *divinity* and *atonement*—with a new meaning, in order *"to deceive, if* [it were] *possible, even the elect"* (Matt. 24:24).

Even the Christian Scientist will tell you that he believes in the Atonement and that the founder of Christian Science, Mary Baker Eddy, taught the Atonement. But when you begin to ask direct and pointed questions regarding his belief and teaching, you will find that by "Atonement" he means, and Mrs. Eddy meant, something entirely different from what you mean and what the Bible teaches. Paul told us that the Devil camouflages himself as *"an angel of light"* (2 Cor. 11:14), but never has he done it more successfully and dangerously than in the

---

* Unitarianism denies the Christian doctrine of the Trinity and the Christian doctrine of the deity of Jesus Christ. Christian Science falsely teaches that disease, sin, death, etc., do not really exist but are the cause of mental error. Its official name is Church of Christ, Scientist.

teaching about the Atonement that he inspired in Mary Baker Eddy and in Unitarian teachers, and also in the teachers in many supposedly Christian pulpits.

Some years ago, I taught a Bible class in Minneapolis, which was attended by people from all the churches in the area. I happened to remark that Christian Science denies the doctrine of the Atonement through the shed blood of Jesus Christ. A very intelligent lady, a lady perfect in her manners, came to me at the close of the class and said, "Mr. Torrey, you should not have said that about Christian Science, for you do not understand its teachings. Christian Scientists do teach the Atonement." I replied, "I said that Christian Science denies the doctrine of the Atonement *through the shed blood of Jesus Christ.* Do you believe, as the Bible states in 1 Peter 2:24, that Jesus Christ bore your sins in His own body on the cross?" She answered, "I think Christian Science is a beautiful system of teaching." I said, "That is not what I asked you. Do you believe that Jesus Christ bore your sins in His own body on the cross?" She replied, "Christian Science has done me a great deal of good." "That is not what I asked you. Do you believe that Jesus Christ bore your sins in His own body on the cross?" "I think that Jesus Christ's life was the most beautiful life ever lived here on earth." "That is not what I asked you. Do you believe that Jesus Christ bore your sins in His own body on the cross?" "The Christian Scientists are lovely people." "But do you believe that Jesus Christ bore your sins in His own body on the cross?" "I believe in following the Lord Jesus Christ." "Do you believe that Jesus

Christ bore your sins in His own body on the cross?" "Oh," she said, "that is a doctrinal question." "Now," I said, "you yourself are an illustration of the truth of the very thing I said. You do not believe in the Atonement *through the shed blood of Jesus Christ.*"

The Christian Scientist uses the word *atonement,* but he means something entirely different from what the Bible teaches regarding the atoning death of Jesus Christ. So does the Unitarian, and so do many of the ministers from supposedly Christian denominations. A pastor in Los Angeles said recently, "I have my own kind of religion. It works for me, but I hope I have enough sense to see that it would not work for everybody. I imagine that if the pastor down the street preached my kind of religious doctrine—without a Devil, without a hell, without an *atonement of blood* and retribution, without an infallible Bible—his audience would melt away like snow in the rain. Is his doctrine truer than mine, or is mine truer than his? Why, neither. His is true for him, and mine is true for me."

Now, his thinking may sound tolerant and lovely, but it is utter nonsense. Any doctrine that is not true for everybody is not true for anybody, and any doctrine that is true is true for everybody. If a doctrine that leaves out an atonement of blood is not true for the pastor down the street—and it certainly is not—then it is not true for anybody else. Truth is not relative; it is absolute. What is true is true, and what is false is false. So we come face to face with the question, What does the Bible teach about this great fundamental doctrine of the Atonement?

The Necessity and Importance of Christ's Death

The first thing that the Bible plainly teaches on this question is the absolute necessity and fundamental importance of the death of Jesus Christ and the shedding of His blood. The tendency in our day in Unitarian circles—and in Christian circles that have been corrupted by Unitarianism—is to minimize the importance of the death of our Lord Jesus Christ. The tendency is to make His life and character, His teaching and leadership, the main thing. Christian Science even goes so far as to deny the fact of His death. To them His death is "an illusion"; it is only "mortal thought." But the Bible puts its emphasis on His atoning death.

Christ's Death Is Referred to Many Times in the Bible

The death of Jesus Christ is mentioned directly more than 175 times in the New Testament. Besides this, there are very many prophetic and typological references to the death of Jesus Christ in the Old Testament.

When I was holding some meetings in the Royal Albert Hall in London, someone took one of our hymnbooks, went through it, and cut out every reference to the blood. Then he sent it back to me through the mail, saying, "I have gone through your hymnbook and cut out every reference to the blood. These references to the blood are foolish. Now sing your hymns with the blood left out, and there will be some sense in them." If you were to take your Bible and go through it that way, cutting out of the New

Testament and Old Testament every passage that refers to the death of Christ or to His atoning blood, you would have a sadly torn and tattered Bible—a Bible without a heart, and a gospel without saving power.

If I were a member of a church where the pastor preached a system of religious doctrine "without a Devil, without a hell, without an atonement of blood and retribution, without an infallible Bible," he would see his own audience "melting away like snow in the rain" as far as I was concerned. Either the pastor would get out of the pulpit, or I would get out of that church, for I would know that he was not preaching God's pure, saving Gospel, but the Devil's poisonous substitute.

Christ's Death Was His Reason for Becoming Man

Not only are the references to the death of Christ so numerous in the Old and New Testaments, but we are taught distinctly in Hebrews 2:14 that Jesus Christ became a man for the specific purpose of dying. He became a partaker of flesh and blood so that He could die. In this verse, we read,

> *Inasmuch then as the children have partaken of flesh and blood, He Himself likewise shared in the same, that through death He might destroy him who had the power of death, that is, the devil.*

The meaning of these words is as plain as day. They tell us that the Incarnation was for the purpose of

Christ's death. They tell us that His death was not a mere accident or incident of His human life (as many would have us believe) but that it was the supreme purpose of it. He became man in order to die as man and for man. This is the doctrine of the Bible, and it is true for anybody and for everybody.

Furthermore, Jesus Christ died for a specific purpose. He died as a ransom for us. He Himself said so in Matthew 20:28: *"The Son of Man did not come to be served, but to serve, and to give His life a ransom for many."*

Christ's Death Was the Topic of Conversation at the Transfiguration

One of the most remarkable scenes recorded in the New Testament is that of the Transfiguration, when Moses and Elijah came back from the other world to commune with Jesus. And what did they talk about in that great moment of human history? Luke 9:30–31 tells us:

> *And behold, two men talked with Him [Jesus], who were Moses and Elijah, who appeared in glory and spoke of His decease which He was about to accomplish at Jerusalem.*

His atoning death was the one subject that engrossed the attention of these two men who came back from the glory world.

We are also told in 1 Peter 1:10–12 that the death of Jesus Christ is a subject of intense interest and earnest inquiry on the part of the angels. We are told that it is something that *"angels desire to look into"* (v. 12).

Christ's Death Is the Theme of Heaven's Song

The death of Christ is the central theme of heaven's song. Revelation 5:8–13 gives us a picture of heaven with its wonderful choir of *"ten thousand times ten thousand, and thousands of thousands,"* and this is a description of the song they sing:

Now when He [the Lamb] had taken the scroll, the four living creatures and the twenty-four elders fell down before the Lamb [Jesus], each having a harp, and golden bowls full of incense, which are the prayers of the saints. And they sang a new song, saying: "You are worthy to take the scroll, and to open its seals; for You were slain, and have redeemed us to God by Your blood out of every tribe and tongue and people and nation, and have made us kings and priests to our God; and we shall reign on the earth." Then I looked, and I heard the voice of many angels around the throne, the living creatures, and the elders; and the number of them was ten thousand times ten thousand, and thousands of thousands, saying with a loud voice: "Worthy is the Lamb who was slain to receive power and riches and wisdom, and strength and honor and glory and blessing!" And every creature which is in heaven and on the earth and under the earth and such as are in the sea, and all that are in them, I heard saying: "Blessing and honor

and glory and power be to Him who sits on the
throne, and to the Lamb, forever and ever!"
(Rev. 5:8–13)

So it is evident that the great central theme of
heaven's song is the atoning death of Jesus Christ,
and the shed *"blood"* by which He redeemed people
"out of every tribe and tongue and people and nation."
If the Unitarian or the Christian Scientist were to go
to heaven, he would have no song to sing. The glorious song of that wondrous choir would sound to him
like a gruesome hymn. He would be very lonesome
and feel that he had sat in the wrong pew.

The Purpose of Christ's Death

We have seen the fundamental and central importance of Christ's death, of the shedding of His
blood. But what was its purpose?

Christ Died as a Vicarious Offering for Sin

First of all, the Bible distinctly and repeatedly
tells us by direct statement, and by countless typological references in the Old Testament, that He
died as a vicarious offering for sin. He, an absolutely
perfect, righteous One who deserved to live, died in
the place of unrighteous men who deserved to die.
For example, we read in Isaiah 53:5,

But He was wounded for our transgressions,
He was bruised for our iniquities; the chas-
tisement for our peace was upon Him, and by
His stripes we are healed.

17

And in the eighth verse, we read,

> *He was taken from prison and from judgment, and who will declare His generation? For He was cut off from the land of the living; for the transgressions of My people He was stricken.*

And in the eleventh and twelfth verses, we read,

> *He shall see the labor of His soul, and be satisfied. By His knowledge My righteous Servant shall justify many, for He shall bear their iniquities. Therefore I will divide Him a portion with the great, and He shall divide the spoil with the strong, because He poured out His soul unto death, and He was numbered with the transgressors, and He bore the sin of many, and made intercession for the transgressors.*

In 1 Peter 3:18, we read,

> *For Christ also suffered once for sins, the just for the unjust, that He might bring us to God, being put to death in the flesh but made alive by the Spirit.*

And in 1 Peter 2:24, we read,

> *Who Himself bore our sins in His own body on the tree, that we, having died to sins, might live for righteousness; by whose stripes you were healed.*

Now, the meaning of these verses and many others is inescapable. No one can misunderstand their message unless he is determined not to see. These verses teach that the death of Jesus Christ was a vicarious atonement. That is, a just One who deserved to live died in the place of unjust ones who deserved to die. His death was, to use the language of the Los Angeles minister who denied any belief in the Atonement, "an atonement of blood and retribution." This is God's doctrine of the Atonement versus the Unitarian and Christian Science doctrine of the Atonement.

Christ Died as a Ransom

But this is not all. We are further taught that Jesus Christ died as a ransom; that is, His death was the price paid to redeem others from death. He Himself said so. His own words are, *"The Son of Man did not come to be served, but to serve, and to give His life a ransom for many"* (Matt. 20:28). If His life was not a ransom—that is to say, if He did not redeem others from death by dying in their place—then He was the greatest fool in the whole history of this universe. Was He a fool, or was He a ransom? No one who in any real sense can be said to believe on the Lord Jesus Christ can hesitate as to his answer.

Christ Died as a Sin Offering

But even this is not all. The Bible distinctly tells us that He died as a sin offering. That is, it was on

the ground of His death—and on this ground alone—
that forgiveness of sin was made possible for and offered to sinners. This we are told in the fifty-third
chapter of Isaiah, to which I have already referred.
In the tenth verse, it is written,

> *Yet it pleased the LORD to bruise Him; He*
> [Jehovah] *has put Him to grief* [literally,
> "made Him sick"]. *When You make His soul*
> *an offering for sin, He shall see His seed, He*
> *shall prolong His days, and the pleasure of the*
> *LORD shall prosper in His hand.*

Now, the meaning of *"an offering for sin"* is unques-
tionable to anyone who has studied the Old Testament offerings. *"An offering for sin,"* or *"a guilt*
offering"—which is the exact meaning of the Hebrew word translated *"an offering for sin"*—was the
death of a sacrificial victim on the ground of which
pardon was offered to sinners. (See Leviticus 6:6–7.)

The Holy Spirit said explicitly in Hebrews 9:22,
"Without shedding of blood there is no remission."
The meaning of these words is unmistakable, and
their force is inescapable. The whole context of Hebrews 9:22 shows that the *"blood,"* to which all the
blood of the Old Testament types as sacrifices
pointed, is the blood of Jesus Christ. So then, the
Word of God declares that apart from the shedding
of the blood of Jesus Christ, there is absolutely no
pardon for sin. There is absolutely no forgiveness
outside of the atoning blood of Christ. If it were not
for Christ's atoning blood, every member of the human race would forever perish.

Christ Died as a Propitiation for Our Sins

Fourth and further yet, the Bible teaches that Jesus Christ died as a *"propitiation for our sins."* God the Father gave Christ the Son to be a *"propitiation by His blood."* That is to say, Jesus Christ, through the shedding of His blood, is the means by which God's holy wrath at sin is appeased. We read in 1 John 4:10, *"In this is love, not that we loved God, but that He loved us and sent His Son to be the propitiation for our sins."* And we read in Romans 3:25–26,

> *Whom God set forth as a propitiation by His blood, through faith, to demonstrate His righteousness, because in His forbearance God had passed over the sins that were previously committed, to demonstrate at the present time His righteousness, that He might be just and the justifier of the one who has faith in Jesus.*

The meaning of these words is also as plain as day. The two Greek words used for *"propitiation"* in these two passages are not exactly the same word, but they are from the same root. The word used for *"propitiation"* in 1 John 4:10 is *hilasmos,* and the word used for *"propitiation"* in Romans 3:25 is *hilasterion.* The definition of *hilasmos* given in *Thayer's Greek-English Lexicon of the New Testament,* which is the standard work, is "the means of appeasing." The definition of *hilasterion* given in the same dictionary is "an expiatory sacrifice." Of course, an expiatory sacrifice is one that makes atonement or satisfaction, one that removes guilt and cancels the obligation to punish the offender. So the thought that is in both passages is that the death of Jesus Christ was a *"propitiation,"* "an expiatory sacrifice," the "means of appeasing" God's holy wrath at sin. In other words, Jesus, through the shedding of His blood, is the means by which the wrath of God against us as sinners is appeased.

God's holiness and consequent hatred of sin, like every other attribute of His character, is real and must manifest itself. His wrath at sin must strike somewhere, either upon the sinner himself or upon a lawful substitute. It struck upon Jesus Christ, a lawful substitute.

As we read in Isaiah 53:6, *"All we like sheep have gone astray; we have turned, every one, to his own way; and the LORD **has laid on Him** [the Lord Jesus] the iniquity of us all"* (emphasis added). The word translated *"has laid,"* according to the marginal note of the Revised Version, means literally, "has made to light." More literally still, it means, "has made to strike." If we read it in this way, what God said through Isaiah is, *"All we like sheep have gone astray; we have turned, every one, to his own way; and the LORD* [has made to strike] *on Him the iniquity of us all."* In the eighth verse of the same chapter, we are taught that the stroke due to others fell upon Jesus Christ, and He was consequently *"cut off from the land of the living."* The first cause of the death of Jesus Christ is the demands of God's holiness.

This is the biblical doctrine versus the Unitarian and Christian Science doctrine of atonement. The biblical doctrine is often misrepresented and distorted

as follows: God, a holy first person, took the sins of
man, the guilty second person, and put them on Jesus Christ, an innocent third person. Those who believe this false viewpoint often say, "This is not
just." No, this would not be just, and it is not for a
moment the doctrine of the Bible. The Bible clearly
teaches that Jesus Christ was not a third person but
was Himself God, and was also man. So He was not a
third person at all, but both the first person and the
second person. The true doctrine of the Atonement
is that God, instead of punishing the sinner for his
sins, took the punishment upon Himself. This act
certainly is something more than justice—it is wondrous love.

Christ Died to Redeem Us from the Curse of the Law

Further yet, the Bible teaches us that Jesus
Christ died to redeem us from the curse of the law
by bearing that curse Himself. We read in Galatians
3:10,

> As many as are of the works of the law are un-
> der the curse; for it is written, "Cursed is every-
> one who does not continue in all things which
> are written in the book of the law, to do them."

So then, every one of us is under the curse of the
broken law, for not one of us has continued *"in all
things which are written in the book of the law, to do
them."* But we read in the thirteenth verse,

> Christ has redeemed us from the curse of the
> law, having become a curse for us [literally,

"in our behalf"] *(for it is written, "Cursed is everyone who hangs on a tree").*

By His crucifixion and death, Christ redeemed us from the curse that we deserved by taking that curse upon Himself. This certainly is "an atonement of blood and retribution."

Christ Died as Our Passover Sacrifice

The Bible puts essentially the same truth in still another way, namely, that Jesus Christ died as our Passover Sacrifice. That is, He died so that His shed blood would serve as the ground upon which God would pass over us and spare us. We read in 1 Corinthians 5:7, *"Christ, our Passover, was sacrificed for us."* Now, what a Passover sacrifice was and what it signified to the Israelites we learn from Exodus 12:12–13. Here the Lord told the children of Israel at the inauguration of the Passover,

> *I will pass through the land of Egypt on that night, and will strike all the firstborn in the land of Egypt, both man and beast; and against all the gods of Egypt I will execute judgment: I am the LORD. Now the blood shall be a sign for you on the houses where you are. And when I see the blood, I will pass over you; and the plague shall not be on you to destroy you when I strike the land of Egypt.*

Again, we read in the twenty-third verse of the same chapter,

> For the LORD will pass through to strike the
> Egyptians; and when He sees the blood on the
> lintel and on the two doorposts, the LORD will
> pass over the door and not allow the destroyer
> to come into your houses to strike you.

Paul wrote his words in 1 Corinthians 5:7 with
all this in mind. When Paul said that Christ is our
Passover Sacrifice, beyond a question he meant that
the shed blood of Jesus Christ serves as a ground—
the only ground—upon which God passes over and
spares us.

The Results of Christ's Death

We have seen, then, the gracious and glorious
purposes of the atoning death of Jesus Christ. What
are the results of that death? They are even more
glorious. I can speak of them only in part.

God Can Deal in Mercy with the Whole World

The first result of the atoning death of Jesus
Christ is that a propitiation is provided for the whole
world. We read in 1 John 2:2, *"He Himself is the
propitiation for our sins, and not for ours only but
also for the whole world."* This plainly means that,
by the death of Jesus Christ, a basis is provided upon
which God can deal in mercy and does deal in mercy
with the whole world. All God's merciful dealings
with man are on the ground of Christ's death. Only
on the ground of Christ's death could God deal in
mercy with any man. God's merciful dealings with

the most ungodly blasphemer or the most blatant atheist are on the ground of the atoning death of Jesus Christ.

Every Person Will Be Raised from the Dead

In the second place, through the atoning death of Jesus Christ, all people will obtain resurrection from the dead. We read in Romans 5:18,

> *Therefore, as through one man's offense* [the trespass of Adam] *judgment came to all men, resulting in condemnation, even so through one Man's righteous act* [Christ's righteous act in dying on the cross in obedience to the will of God] *the free gift came to all men, resulting in justification of life.*

Also, we are told in 1 Corinthians 15:22, *"As in Adam all die, even so in Christ all shall be made alive."* In the entire fifteenth chapter of 1 Corinthians, the apostle Paul was speaking about the resurrection of the body, not about eternal life. Here he distinctly taught that even as every child of Adam loses life (physical life—see Genesis 3:19) in the First Adam, so also he obtains resurrection from the dead through the atoning death of Jesus Christ, the Second Adam.

Every person, the most ungodly infidel as well as the most devout believer, will someday be raised from the dead because Christ died in his place. Whether the resurrection that he obtains through the death of Jesus Christ will be a *"resurrection of*

life" or a *"resurrection of condemnation"* (John
5:29), of *"shame and everlasting contempt"* (Dan.
12:2), will depend entirely on what attitude the individual takes toward the Christ in whom he receives
the resurrection.

Every Believer Is Forgiven of Every Sin

By the atoning death of Jesus Christ, all believers in Jesus Christ have forgiveness of all their sins.
We read in Ephesians 1:7, *"In Him* [Jesus Christ] *we
have redemption through His blood, the forgiveness
of sins, according to the riches of His grace."* Because
Jesus Christ died as a full satisfaction for our sins,
forgiveness of sin is not something that believers can
do something to secure. It is something that the
blood of Jesus Christ has already secured and that
our faith has already taken hold of. We *have* forgiveness; we *are* forgiven. Every believer in Jesus Christ
is forgiven of every sin he has ever committed or
ever will commit, because Jesus Christ shed His
blood in his place.

As we read in Romans 5:10, *"When we were
enemies we were reconciled to God through the death
of His Son."* Through Christ's atoning death, all believers in Him, although they once *"were enemies,"*
are now *"reconciled to God through the death of His
Son."* That is to say, the enmity between God and
the sinner is done away with, or, as Paul put it in
Colossians 1:20, Christ has *"made peace through the
blood of His cross."* Or, as he put it in the next two
verses, Christ *"has reconciled* [believers] *in the body
of His flesh through death"* (Col. 1:21–22).

27

The story is told of a faithful English minister in the 1800s who was told that one of his parishioners was dying. She was a good woman, and he hurried to her side to talk with her. As he sat down beside the dying woman, he said to her very gently but solemnly, "They tell me you do not have long to live." "No," she replied, "I know I do not." "They tell me you will probably not live through the night." "No," she replied, "I do not expect to live through the night." Then he said very earnestly, "Have you made your peace with God?" She replied, "No, I have not." "And are you not afraid to meet God without having made your peace with Him?" "No, not at all," she calmly replied.

Again, he said to her, "Do you understand what I am saying? Do you realize that you are at the point of death?" "Yes." "Do you realize you probably will not live through the night?" "Yes." "And you have not made your peace with God?" "No." "And you are not afraid to meet Him?" "No, not at all."

Something about the woman's manner made him think there was something behind her words, and so he asked, "What do you mean?" She replied, "I know I am dying and will not live through the night. I know I must soon meet God, and I am not at all disturbed. I did not need to make my peace with God, because Jesus Christ made peace with God for me more than eighteen hundred years ago by His death on the cross of Calvary. I am resting in the peace that Jesus Christ has already made."

The woman was right. No one needs to make his or her peace with God; Jesus Christ has already made peace by His atoning death, and all we have to do is enter into the peace that Jesus Christ has made for us. We enter into that peace by simply believing in the One who made peace by His death on the cross. Jesus Christ's work was a complete and perfect work. There is nothing to be added to it. We cannot add anything to it, and we do not need to. Jesus Christ has *"made peace through the blood of His cross"* (Col. 1:20).

Every Believer Is Justified

The fourth result of the atoning death of Jesus Christ is that all believers in Him are justified. We read in Romans 5:9, *"Having now been justified by His blood."*

Justification is more than forgiveness. Forgiveness is the putting away of our sins, which is manifested in God's treating us as if we had never sinned. Justification means to count us as positively righteous, to impute to us the perfect righteousness of God in Jesus Christ. God does not merely treat us as if we had never sinned, but He sees us as clothed with perfect righteousness.

Because of Jesus Christ's atoning death, there is an absolute exchange of position between Jesus Christ and His people. In His death on the cross, Jesus Christ took our place of condemnation before God; and the moment we accept Him, we step into His place of perfect acceptance before God. As Paul put it in 2 Corinthians 5:21, *"He made Him who knew no sin to be sin for us, that we might become the righteousness of God in Him."* Jesus Christ stepped into our place in the curse and rejection, and the moment we accept Him, we step into His place of perfect acceptance.

This truth has been expressed by one poet as follows:

> Near, so very near to God,
>   Nearer I cannot be;
> For in the person of His Son,
>   I'm just as near as He.
>
> Dear, so very dear to God,
>   Dearer I cannot be;
> For in the person of His Son,
>   I'm just as dear as He.

Every Believer Has Bold Access into God's Presence

Furthermore, because of the full atonement that Jesus Christ has made by the shedding of His blood, every believer can enter boldly into the Holy Place, into the very presence of God. As it is put in Hebrews 10:19–22,

> *Therefore, brethren, having boldness to enter the Holiest* [the very presence of God] *by the blood of Jesus, by a new and living way which He consecrated for us, through the veil, that is, His flesh, and having a High Priest over the house of God, let us draw near with a true heart in full assurance of faith.*

Some of us hesitate to come into the presence of God when we think of the greatness and the number of our sins and when we think of how holy God is.

30

Even the seraphim (the "burning ones," burning in their own intense holiness) veil their faces and feet in His presence and unceasingly cry, *"Holy, holy, holy is the LORD of hosts"* (Isa. 6:3).

We say to ourselves, "God is holy." Yes. "And I am a sinner." Yes. But by the wondrous offering of Christ *"once for all"* (Heb. 10:10), I am *"perfected forever"* (v. 14). On the ground of that blood—so precious and so sufficient in God's eyes—I can march boldly into the very presence of God, look up with unveiled face into His face, call Him Father, and pour out before Him every desire of my heart. (See Hebrews 4:16.) Oh, wondrous blood!

Every Believer Obtains Eternal Life and an Eternal Inheritance

But this is not all. Because of the atoning death of Jesus Christ, those who believe in Him will live with Him forever. How plainly Paul put it in 1 Thessalonians 5:9–10: *"Our Lord Jesus Christ... died for us, that...we should live together with Him."*

Further yet, because of the atoning death of Jesus Christ, all those who believe in Him *"receive the promise of the eternal inheritance."* This is what we are told in Hebrews 9:15:

> And for this reason He is the Mediator of the new covenant, by means of death, for the redemption of the transgressions under the first covenant, that those who are called may receive the promise of the eternal inheritance.

If I had more time, I would go into greater detail about this wonderful promise.

The Material Universe Is Reconciled to God

There are results of the atoning death and resurrection of Jesus Christ regarding His victory over the Devil and his angels, which we are not able to cover here. I will cover just one more thing: the results of His atoning death concerning the material universe. God teaches us that, through the death of Jesus Christ, the material universe—*"all things,... whether things on earth or things in heaven"*—is reconciled to God. These are His words:

> For it pleased the Father that in Him [Jesus Christ] all the fullness should dwell, and by Him to reconcile all things to Himself, by Him, whether things on earth or things in heaven, having made peace through the blood of His cross.   (Col. 1:19–20)

These are wonderful words. They tell us that the death of Jesus Christ is related to the material universe, to things on earth and to things in heaven, as well as to us and to our sins.

The material universe has fallen away from God in connection with sin. (See Genesis 3:17–18; Romans 8:20.) Both earth and heaven have been invaded and polluted by sin. (See Ephesians 6:12; Hebrews 9:23–24.) Through the death of Jesus Christ, this pollution is put away. Just as the blood of the Old Testament sacrifice was taken into the

Most Holy Place of the temple, the type of heaven, so Christ has taken the blood of the better sacrifice into heaven itself and cleansed it. *"All things,...whether things on earth or things in heaven"* (Col. 1:20), are now reconciled to God. *"The creation itself also will be delivered from the bondage of corruption into the glorious liberty of the children of God"* (Rom. 8:21). *"We...look for new heavens and a new earth in which righteousness dwells"* (2 Pet. 3:13).

The atonement of Jesus Christ has an immense sweep, far beyond the reach of our human philosophies. We have just begun to understand what the blood that was spilled on Calvary means. Sin is a far more awful, ruinous, and far-reaching evil than we have been accustomed to thinking, but the blood of Christ has power and effectiveness, the fullness of which only eternity will disclose.

Two

Am I Justified by My Good Works?

Am I Justified by My Good Works?

Therefore let it be known to you, brethren, that through this Man is preached to you the forgiveness of sins; and by Him everyone who believes is justified from all things from which you could not be justified by the law of Moses.
—Acts 13:38–39

But to him who does not work but believes on Him who justifies the ungodly, his faith is accounted for righteousness.
—Romans 4:5

These are two remarkable passages, and I will explain them both in this chapter. Our subject is justification by faith, which is the distinctive doctrine of Protestantism, for it was the central tenet of the Reformation. Today, this teaching is one of the vital doctrines of evangelicalism. The first biblical writer to fully explain and repeatedly emphasize this teaching was Paul. However, it can be found throughout the entire Bible, from Genesis to Revelation. In the first book of the Bible, we read,

"[Abraham] *believed in the LORD, and He accounted it to him for righteousness*" (Gen. 15:6). In these words, we have the seed of the gracious and precious doctrine of justification by faith.

What Is Justification?

The first thing for us to understand is what justification is. At this point, many people go astray in their study of this great truth. There are two fundamentally different definitions of the words *justify* and *justification*. One definition of justify is "to make righteous," and of justification, "being made righteous." The other definition of justify is "to count, declare, or show to be righteous," and of justification, "being declared or counted righteous." Based on these two different definitions, two different schools of thought depart from one another. Which is the true definition?

The way to settle the meaning of any word in the Bible is by examining all the passages in which that word and its derivatives are found. If anyone will go through the Bible, the Old Testament and the New, and carefully study all the passages in which the word *justify* and its derivatives are found, he will discover that, beyond a question, the biblical definition of justify is not "to make righteous," but "to count righteous, declare righteous, or show to be righteous." A person is justified before God when God counts him righteous.

This truth appears, for example, in Romans 4:2–8:

> *For if Abraham was justified by works, he has something to boast about, but not before God.*

> *For what does the Scripture say? "Abraham
> believed God, and it was accounted to him for
> righteousness." Now to him who works, the
> wages are not counted as grace but as debt.
> But to him who does not work but believes on
> Him who justifies the ungodly, his faith is ac-
> counted for righteousness, just as David also
> describes the blessedness of the man to whom
> God imputes righteousness apart from works:
> "Blessed are those whose lawless deeds are
> forgiven, and whose sins are covered; blessed
> is the man to whom the LORD shall not impute
> sin."*

It is plain from this passage, and from many others,
that a person is justified when God counts him
righteous, no matter what his character and conduct
may have been. Of course, as we saw in the previous
chapter and will see again later in this chapter, justification means more than mere forgiveness.

How Are We Justified?

Now we come to the second question, which is
the all-important question: How are we justified? In
general, there are two opposing views of justification. The first view states that people are justified by
their own works, that is, on the ground of something
that they themselves do. This view may be expressed
in various ways. The good works that people speak of
as the ground of their justification may be their good
moral conduct or their keeping of the Golden Rule or
something of that sort. Or, they may be works of religion, such as doing penance, saying prayers, joining

the church, going to church, being baptized, partaking of the Lord's Supper, or performing some other religious duty. But these all amount to the same thing: in their view, it is something that they themselves do that brings justification.

The other view of justification is that we are justified not by our own works in any sense, but entirely by the work of Another, that is, by the atoning death of Jesus Christ on the cross of Calvary. This view states that our own works have nothing to do with our justification but that we are justified entirely by Christ's finished and complete work of atonement. Furthermore, all that we have to do to receive our justification is merely to take hold of it by simply trusting in the One who made the atonement.

Which is the correct view? We will go directly to the Bible for the answer to this all-important question.

We Are Not Justified by Our Own Works

We find the first part of the answer in Romans 3:20: *"Therefore by the deeds of the law no flesh will be justified in His sight, for by the law is the knowledge of sin."* Here it is very plainly stated that we are not justified by keeping the law of God, either the Mosaic Law or any other law. The law is given, not to bring us justification, but to bring us a knowledge of sin, that is, to bring us to the realization of our need of justification by grace. In the above verse, it is plainly stated that no one is justified by the works of the law. The same great truth is found in Galatians 2:16:

> *Knowing that a man is not justified by the*
> *works of the law but by faith in Jesus Christ,*
> *even we have believed in Christ Jesus, that we*
> *might be justified by faith in Christ and not by*
> *the works of the law; for by the works of the*
> *law no flesh shall be justified.*

Justification by any works of our own is an impossibility. Why? Because in order to be justified by the works of the law, or by anything we can do, we must keep the law of God perfectly. The law demands perfect obedience as the ground of justification. It says, *"Cursed is everyone who does not continue in all things which are written in the book of the law, to do them"* (Gal. 3:10). But not one of us has perfectly kept the law of God, and the moment we break the law of God at any point, justification by works becomes an absolute impossibility. Therefore, as far as the law of God is concerned, every one of us is under the curse, and if we are to be justified at all, we must find some other way of justification than by keeping the law of God.

God did not give mankind the law with the expectation or intention that they would keep it and be justified by it. He gave them the law in order to produce conviction of sin and to lead them to Christ. Or, as Paul put it in Romans 3:19–20,

> *Now we know that whatever the law says, it*
> *says to those who are under the law, that every*
> *mouth may be stopped, and all the world may*
> *become guilty before God. Therefore by the*

*deeds of the law no flesh will be justified in His
sight, for by the law is the knowledge of sin.*

These words of God are plain. But strangely enough,
many people today are preaching the law as a way of
salvation. When they preach this message, they are
preaching another way of salvation than the one laid
down in God's own Word.

We Are Justified Freely by God's Grace

The answer to the question of how we are justified has a second part. We find it in Romans 3:24:
*"Being justified freely by His grace through the re-
demption that is in Christ Jesus."* The word translated *"freely"* in this passage means "as a free gift."
This verse tells us that justification is a free gift by
God's grace (God's unmerited favor) *"through* [on
the ground of] *the redemption that is in Christ Jesus."* In other words, justification is not on the
ground of any merit that is in us or anything that we
have done. We are justified neither by our own doing
nor by our own character. Justification is an absolutely free gift; God bestows it without asking for
payment. The channel through which this free gift is
bestowed is *"the redemption that is in Christ Jesus."*
Christ paid the purchase price of our redemption by
shedding His blood on Calvary's cross.

We Are Justified by Christ's Shed Blood

The third part of the answer is found in Romans
5:9: *"Much more then, having now been justified by*

His blood, we shall be saved from wrath through Him." Here we are told in so many words that we are *"justified,"* or counted righteous, *"by,"* or more literally, "in," Christ's *"blood"*—that is, on the ground of Christ's propitiatory death. We were all under the curse of the broken law of God, for we had all broken it. But by dying in our place on the cross of Calvary, our Lord Jesus Christ *"has redeemed us from the curse of the law, having become a curse for us (for it is written, 'Cursed is everyone who hangs on a tree')"* (Gal. 3:13).

Peter put it this way in 1 Peter 2:24: "[Christ] *Himself bore our sins in His own body on the tree."* Paul put it this way in 2 Corinthians 5:21: "[God] *made Him* [Christ] *who knew no sin to be sin for us, that we might become the righteousness of God in Him."* We will have the opportunity to come back to this passage later. All that I want you to notice in it right now is that it is on the ground of Jesus Christ's becoming a substitute for us, on the ground of His taking the place we deserved on the cross, that we are counted righteous. The one and only ground of justification is the shed blood of Jesus Christ.

Of course, this doctrine is entirely different from the teaching of Christian Science, and entirely different from the teaching of New Thought and Theosophy,* and entirely different from the teaching of

---

* New Thought teaches that the power of the mind can achieve health and happiness. Its teachings are similar to those of Christian Science. Theosophy is the teachings of a movement that originated in the U.S. in 1875 and that follows primarily Buddhistic and Hindu theories, especially of pantheistic evolution and reincarnation.

Unitarianism. But it is the teaching of the Word of God. We find this same teaching clearly given by the prophet Isaiah seven hundred years before our Lord was born:

> *All we like sheep have gone astray; we have turned, every one, to his own way; and the LORD has laid* [literally, "made to strike"] *on Him* [the Lord Jesus] *the iniquity of us all.*
> *(Isa. 53:6)*

Get this point clearly settled in your mind: the sole but all-sufficient ground upon which people are justified before God is the shed blood of Jesus Christ. He offered His blood as an atonement for our sins, and God the Father accepted it as an all-sufficient atonement.

We Are Justified by Faith in Jesus

The fourth part of the answer to the question of how we are justified is in Romans 3:26:

> *To demonstrate at the present time His* [God's] *righteousness, that He* [God] *might be just and the justifier of the one who has faith in Jesus.*

Here we are taught that we are justified on the condition of faith in Jesus. If possible, Romans 4:5 makes this even plainer: *"To him who does not work but believes on Him who justifies the ungodly, his faith is accounted for righteousness."* Here the Holy Spirit, speaking through the apostle Paul, tells us that the faith of those who believe in Jesus *"is accounted for righteousness."* In other words, faith makes Christ's shed blood, which is the ground of justification, ours. We are justified when we believe.

Every person is *potentially* justified by the death of Christ on the cross, but believers are *actually* justified by taking hold of the justifying value in His shed blood by faith. Simple faith in Jesus Christ is the sole condition of justification. God asks nothing else of the sinner than that he believe in His Son, Jesus Christ. When he believes, he is justified, whether he has any works to offer or not. As Paul put it in Romans 3:28, *"Therefore we conclude that a man is justified by faith apart from the deeds of the law."* Or, as Paul put it in the verse already quoted, *"To him who does not work but believes on Him who justifies the ungodly, his faith is accounted for righteousness"* (Rom. 4:5).

A person is justified entirely apart from the works of the law. That is, he is justified on the condition that he believe in Jesus Christ, even though he has no works to offer as the ground upon which to claim justification. When we cease to work for justification and simply believe *"on Him who justifies the ungodly,"* our faith is *"accounted for righteousness,"* and therefore we are accounted righteous.

The question, then, is not, Do you have any works to offer? but, Do you believe in the One who justifies the ungodly? Works have nothing to do with justification, except to hinder it when we trust in them. The blood of Jesus Christ secures justification; faith in Jesus Christ takes hold of it. We are justified not by our works, but by His work. We are justified on the simple and single ground of His shed blood and on the simple and single condition of our faith in the One who shed the blood.

So great is the pride of the natural heart that it is extremely difficult to hold people to this doctrine of justification by faith apart from the works of the law. We are constantly seeking to bring in our own works somewhere.

We Are Justified by a Heart-Faith That Confesses Christ

But I have not yet completely answered the question of how we are justified. There is another side to the truth, and if our doctrine of justification is to be complete and well-balanced, we must look at this other side. We will find part of it in Romans 10:9–10:

> *If you confess with your mouth the Lord Jesus and believe in your heart that God has raised Him from the dead, you will be saved. For with the heart one believes unto righteousness, and with the mouth confession is made unto salvation.*

Here God tells us that the faith that takes hold of justification is a faith of the heart. This faith is not a mere idea or opinion; this faith leads to action. This faith leads to open, verbal confession of Jesus as Lord.

If a person has a faith, or what he calls a faith, that does not lead him to an open confession of Christ, he has a faith that does not justify; it is not a faith of the heart. Our Lord Jesus Christ Himself told us that heart-faith leads to open confession, for He said in Matthew 12:34, *"Out of the abundance of the heart the mouth speaks."* Heart-faith in Jesus Christ inevitably leads to a verbal confession of Jesus as Lord. If you are not confessing Jesus as your Lord with your mouth, you do not have justifying faith, and you are not justified.

We Are Justified by a Faith That Works

Let us examine the rest of this other side of the truth. James 2:14 says, *"What doth it profit, my brethren, if a man say he hath faith, but have not works? can that faith save him?"* (RV). We see here that a faith that a person merely says he has, but that does not lead to works consistent with what he claims to believe, cannot justify. James went on to say in verses 18–24,

> But someone will say, *"You have faith, and I have works."* Show me your faith without your works, and I will show you my faith by my works. You believe that there is one God. You do well. Even the demons believe; and tremble! But do you want to know, O foolish man, that faith without works is dead? Was not Abraham our father justified by works when he offered Isaac his son on the altar? Do you see that faith was working together with his works, and by works faith was made perfect? [That is, in the works to which Abraham's faith led, faith had its perfect manifestation.] And the Scripture was fulfilled which says,

> *"Abraham believed God, and it was accounted to him for righteousness." And he was called the friend of God. You see then that a man is justified by works, and not by faith only.*
> *(James 2:18–24)*

Some see in these verses a contradiction between the teaching of James and the teaching of Paul, but there is no contradiction whatsoever. Here James taught us an important truth, namely, that the faith that one says he has, but that does not manifest itself in action, will not justify. The faith that justifies is real faith that leads to actions consistent with the truth we profess to believe. It is true that we are justified simply by faith apart from the works of the law, *but our faith must be real faith;* otherwise, it does not justify. As someone once put it, "We are justified by faith without works, but we are not justified by a faith that is without works."

The faith that God sees and upon which He justifies leads inevitably to works that others can see. God saw the faith of Abraham the moment Abraham believed, before there was any opportunity to work, and He accounted that faith to Abraham for righteousness. But the faith that God saw was a real faith, and it led Abraham to works that all could see. These works proved the reality of his faith. To us, the proof of the faith is the works, and we know that he who does not work does not have justifying faith.

On the one hand, we must not lose sight of the truth that Paul emphasized to combat legalism, namely, that we are justified on the single and simple condition of a real faith in Christ. But on the other hand, we must not lose sight of the truth that James emphasized to combat lawless living, namely, that a justifying faith is a real faith that proves its genuineness by works. To the legalist who is seeking to do something to merit justification, we must say, "Stop working, and believe in the One who justifies the ungodly." (See Romans 4:5.) To the one who thinks he can live a lawless, careless, unseparated, sinful life and still be justified—the one who boasts that he has faith and is justified by it but does not show his faith by his works—we must say, *"What doth it profit, my brethren, if a man **say** he hath faith, but have not works? can **that** faith save him?"* (James 2:14 RV, emphasis added). We are justified by faith alone; however, we are not justified by a faith that is alone, but by a faith that is demonstrated by works.

To What Extent Are We Justified?

I think that the above Scriptures have made it plain just how a person is justified. Now we come to another question: To what extent is an individual who believes in the Lord Jesus justified? This question is plainly, wonderfully, and gloriously answered in Acts 13:38–39:

Therefore let it be known to you, brethren, that through this Man is preached to you the forgiveness of sins; and by Him everyone who believes is justified from all things from which you could not be justified by the law of Moses.

These words very plainly declare to us that every believer in Jesus Christ is *"justified from all things."* In other words, the old account against the believer is totally wiped out. No matter how bad and how black the account is, the moment a person believes in Jesus Christ, the account is wiped out. God has absolutely nothing that He counts against the one who believes in Jesus Christ. Even if he is still a very imperfect believer, a very young and immature Christian, he is perfectly justified. As Paul put it in Romans 8:1, *"There is therefore now no condemnation to those who are in Christ Jesus."* Or, as he put it further along in the chapter,

> *Who shall bring a charge against God's elect? It is God who justifies. Who is he who condemns? It is Christ who died, and furthermore is also risen, who is even at the right hand of God, who also makes intercession for us.*
> *(Rom. 8:33–34)*

Suppose the world's most brutal murderer were to hear the gospel of God's grace, believe in the Lord Jesus Christ, and accept Him as his Savior, surrendering to Him and confessing Him as his Lord. The moment he did so, every sin he ever committed would be blotted out, and his record would be as white in God's sight as that of the purest angel in heaven. God counts absolutely nothing against the believer in Jesus Christ.

But this is not all. Paul went beyond this in 2 Corinthians 5:21: "[God] *made Him* [Jesus Christ] *who knew no sin to be sin for us, that we might become the righteousness of God in Him."* Here we are explicitly told that the believer in Jesus Christ is made the *"righteousness of God"* in Christ. In Philippians 3:9, we are told that when one is in Christ, he has a righteousness not his own, a *"righteousness which is from God by faith."* In other words, there is an absolute exchange of positions between Christ and the justified believer. Christ took our place, the place of the curse on the cross (Gal. 3:13). He was *"made to be sin on our behalf"* (2 Cor. 5:21 RV). God counted Him a sinner and dealt with Him as a sinner, causing Him to cry out as He died in the sinner's place, *"My God, My God, why have You forsaken Me?"* (Matt. 27:46). And when we are justified, we step into Christ's place, the place of perfect acceptance before God. In the exact words of Scripture, we *"become the righteousness of God in Him"* (2 Cor. 5:21).

To be justified is more than to be forgiven. Forgiveness is the putting away of sin. Justification is the attributing of perfect righteousness to the one justified. Jesus Christ is so united to the believer that God attributes the believer's sins to Christ. On the other hand, the believer is so united to Christ that God attributes Christ's righteousness to him. God sees us, not as we are in ourselves, but as we are in Him. God considers us to be as righteous as Christ is.

When Christ's work in us has been completed, we will be in actual fact what we are already in God's eyes. However, the moment one believes, as far as God's estimation is concerned, he is as perfect as he ever will be. Our present standing before God is absolutely perfect, though our present state may be very imperfect. Allow me to use again the words of the poet:

> Near, so very near to God,
> Nearer I cannot be;
> For in the person of His Son,
> I'm just as near as He.

> Dear, so very dear to God,
> Dearer I cannot be;
> For in the person of His Son,
> I'm just as dear as He.

When Are We Justified?

One question still remains, though it has really been answered in what has already been said. It concerns the time of justification. When is a believer justified? This question is answered plainly in one of our texts: *"And by Him everyone who believes is justified from all things from which you could not be justified by the law of Moses"* (Acts 13:39). What I want you to particularly notice now in this verse is the word *"is"*: *"Everyone who believes is justified from all things."* This verse plainly answers the question as to when a believer is justified. In Christ Jesus, everyone who believes in Him is justified from all things the moment he believes. The moment a person believes in Jesus Christ, that moment he becomes united to Christ, and God attributes His righteousness to him.

I repeat: if the world's most brutal murderer were to believe in the Lord Jesus Christ, the moment that he did so, not only would every sin he ever committed be blotted out, but all the perfect righteousness of God in Christ would be put in his account. His standing before God would be as perfect as it would be after being in heaven ten million years.

I was preaching one Sunday morning in D. L. Moody's church in Chicago on Romans 8:1, *"There is therefore now no condemnation to those who are in Christ Jesus."* In the course of my preaching, I said, "If the wickedest woman in Chicago were to come into the Chicago Avenue Church this morning and here and now accept Jesus Christ as her Savior, the moment she did so, every sin she ever committed would be blotted out, and her record would be as white in God's sight as that of the purest woman in the auditorium."

Unknown to me, one of the members of my congregation had gone down that very morning into a low den of iniquity near the river and had invited a woman who was an outcast to come and hear me preach. The woman replied, "I never go to church. Church is not for the likes of me. I would not be welcome at the church if I did go." The saintly woman's reply was, "You would be welcome at our church," which, thank God, was true. "No," the woman insisted, "it would not do for me to go to church. Church is not for the likes of me." But the saintly woman urged the sinful woman to go. She offered to accompany her to the church, but the sinful woman said, "No, that would never do. The policemen know me, and the boys on the street know me and sometimes throw stones at me. If they saw you going up the street with me, they would think that you are what I am." But the saintly woman had the Spirit of the Master and said, "I don't care what they think of me. If you will accompany me to hear Mr. Torrey preach, I will go along with you." The other woman refused. But the saved woman was so insistent that the woman who was an outcast finally said, "If you will go up the street a few steps ahead, I will follow you."

Up La Salle Avenue they went, the woman who was a saint a few steps ahead, and the woman who was a sinner a few steps behind. Block after block they went, until they reached the corner of La Salle Avenue and Chicago Avenue. The saved woman entered the tower door at the corner, went up the steps, and entered the church, and the woman who was a sinner followed her. Upon reaching the door, the sinful woman looked in, saw a vacant seat under the balcony in the very last row at the back, and slipped into it. Scarcely had she taken her seat, when I made the remark that I just quoted: "If the wickedest woman in Chicago were to come into the Chicago Avenue Church this morning and here and now accept Jesus Christ as her Savior, the moment she did so, every sin she ever committed would be blotted out, and her record would be as white in God's sight as that of the purest woman in the auditorium." My words went floating down over the audience and dropped into the heart of the sinful woman. She believed them. She believed that Jesus died for her. She believed that by the shedding of His blood she could be saved. Believing, she found pardon and peace and justification then and there. When the meeting was over, she came up the aisle to the front as I stepped down from the pulpit, tears streaming down her face, and thanked me for the blessing that she had received.

I repeat it right now, not knowing who may be reading this, not knowing what may be the secret life of anyone who is reading, not knowing what may be the sins that are hidden in the heart: Even if you are the wickedest man or woman on earth, if you were to here and now accept Jesus Christ as Savior, the moment you did so, every sin you ever committed would be blotted out. In an instant, your record would be as white in God's sight, not only as that of the purest person in the world, but as that of the purest angel in heaven. Not only that, but all the perfect righteousness of God that clothed our Lord Jesus Christ would be put in your account, and you would be just as near and just as dear to God as the Lord Jesus Christ Himself is. That is the doctrine of justification by faith. Wondrous doctrine! Glorious doctrine!

Three

Have I Been Born Again?

Have I Been Born Again?

Jesus answered and said to him, "Most assuredly, I say to you, unless one is born again, he cannot see the kingdom of God....Most assuredly, I say to you, unless one is born of water and the Spirit, he cannot enter the kingdom of God."
—John 3:3, 5

O ur subject in this chapter is regeneration, or the new birth. What I have to say will be covered under four main questions: What does it mean to be born again? What are the results of being born again? Why is it necessary to be born again? How can a person be born again?

What Does It Mean to Be Born Again?

Many people speak of the new birth or of regeneration without any definite idea of just what the new birth is. As a result, they are never sure whether they themselves have been born again or not. In 2 Peter 1:4, we find as clear a definition of the new birth as can be found in the Word of God:

Exceedingly great and precious promises [have been given to us], *that through these you may be partakers of the divine nature, having escaped the corruption that is in the world through lust.*

From these words of Peter, it is evident that the new birth means that a new nature is given to the one who is born again—God's own nature. By being born again, we become actual partakers of the divine nature.

We are all born into this world with a corrupted intellectual and moral nature. The natural person, or unregenerate person, is intellectually blind—blind to the truth of God. He cannot see or receive *"the things of the Spirit"* (1 Cor. 2:14). *"They are foolishness to him; nor can he know them"* (v. 14). His inclinations are corrupt; he loves the things he ought to hate and hates the things he ought to love. A definite description of the inclinations and tastes and desires of the unregenerate person is found in Galatians 5:19–21. He is also perverse in his will, as Paul put it in Romans 8:7: *"The carnal mind is enmity against God; for it is not subject to the law of God, nor indeed can be."* This state of spiritual blindness and moral corruption is the condition of every unregenerate person. No matter how cultured or refined or moral he may be outwardly, his inner life is radically wrong.

In the new birth, God imparts His own wise and holy nature, a nature that thinks as God thinks. The one who is born again *"is renewed in knowledge according to the image of Him who created him"* (Col.

60

3:10). He feels as God feels (1 Cor. 2:16), loves what God loves (1 John 3:14; 4:7–8), hates what God hates (Rev. 2:6), and wills as God wills (Phil. 2:13). It is evident, then, that regeneration is a deep, thorough change in the deepest springs of thought, feeling, and action. It is a change so thorough that Paul said in 2 Corinthians 5:17, *"If anyone is in Christ, he is a new creation; old things have passed away; behold, all things have become new."*

In the inspired language of the apostle John, regeneration is a passing *"out of death into life"* (1 John 3:14 RV). Until we are born again, we are in a condition of moral and spiritual death. When we are born again, we are made alive, we who *"were dead in* [our] *trespasses and sins"* (Eph. 2:1).

There is a profound contrast between true regeneration and a mere conversion experience. Conversion is an outward thing, a turning around. A person is facing the wrong way, facing away from God, and he turns around and faces toward God. That is conversion. But regeneration is not a mere outward change; it is a thorough change in the deepest depths of one's being. It leads to a genuine conversion, or genuine outward change. Many an apparently thorough conversion is a temporary thing because it did not go deep enough; but regeneration is a permanent thing. When God imparts His nature to a person, that nature abides in the person. When he is born again, he cannot be unborn, or as John put it in 1 John 3:9, *"Whoever has been born of God does not sin, for His* [God's] *seed remains in him."* A person may be "converted" a thousand times, but he can be regenerated only once.

What Are the Results of Being Born Again?

Now we come to the second question, which is closely related to the first. It will help us to understand even more clearly what the new birth is. The question is, What are the results of being born again? They are numerous.

We Become the Temple of the Holy Spirit

The first of these results is found in 1 Corinthians 6:19: *"Do you not know that your body is the temple of the Holy Spirit who is in you, whom you have from God?"* These words were spoken to believers, to regenerated individuals, and they plainly tell us that when one is born again, the Holy Spirit comes to take up His permanent dwelling in the person. In this way, the person who is born again becomes a *"temple of the Holy Spirit."* It is true that he may not always be conscious of this indwelling of the Holy Spirit; nevertheless, He dwells in him.

We Are Free from the Law of Sin and Death

The second result of the new birth is found in Romans 8:2–4:

For the law of the Spirit of life in Christ Jesus has made me free from the law of sin and death. For what the law could not do in that it was weak through the flesh, God did by sending His own Son in the likeness of sinful flesh,

*on account of sin: He condemned sin in the
flesh, that the righteous requirement of the law
might be fulfilled in us who do not walk according to the flesh but according to the Spirit.*

In the seventh chapter of Romans, we have a
picture of the person who is awakened by the law of
God. He approves God's law in the *"inward man"*
(Rom. 7:22) and sees it as *"holy and just and good"*
(v. 12). He tries to keep it in his own strength but
utterly fails. At last he comes to the end of himself
and is filled with despair—he despairs of ever being
able to keep the law of God that is outside him because of the law of sin and death that is inside him.
The law of sin and death says, "The good that you
want to do you cannot do, and the evil that you hate
and do not want to do, you must keep on doing."
(See Romans 7:15.)

When a person sees his own utter helplessness,
turns to God, and accepts Jesus Christ, the Holy
Spirit sets him free from this law of sin and death.
By the power of the indwelling Spirit, whom Jesus
Christ gives to the one who dwells in Him, the believer is enabled to obey the law of God. He gets victory over the evil things that he does not want to do,
and he is enabled to do the things that he wants to
do. In a person merely awakened by the law of God,
"the law of sin and death" (Rom. 8:2) gets a perpet-
ual victory. But in a regenerate person, *"the law of
the Spirit of life in Christ Jesus"* (v. 2) gets a perpet-
ual victory.

Undoubtedly, many of you reading this are still
struggling to keep the law of God and are utterly

failing in your attempt to do so. What you need is to be born again and thus have the Holy Spirit come to dwell in you. Then you need to walk by the Spirit. (See Romans 8:1, 4.) By the power of this indwelling Spirit, you can get victory every day and every hour over the law of sin and death that wars in your members against the law of God (Rom. 7:22–23).

We Are Transformed

The third result of the new birth is found in Romans 12:2: *"And do not be conformed to this world, but be transformed by the renewing of your mind."* From this we see that the third result of the new birth is an outward transformation of our lives by an inward renewing of our minds. We are no longer conformed to this world.

Of course, the regenerated person does not immediately have a perfect manifestation of all that is in him in seed form. He begins the new life just as we begin our natural lives, as a babe, and he must grow. As Peter put it in 1 Peter 2:2, we must *"as newborn babes, desire the pure milk of the word, that [we] may grow thereby."* This new life must be fed and developed.

It is irrational and unwarranted by the Word of God to expect someone who has just been born again—someone who is a babe in Christ—to be as perfect in character as someone who was born again years ago and has grown to maturity. But the moment we are born again, we receive in seed all the moral perfection that is to be ours when this seed is fully developed within us and comes to its perfect manifestation.

We Believe That Jesus Is the Christ

The fourth result of the new birth is found in
1 John 5:1: *"Whoever believes that Jesus is the Christ
is born of God."* The fourth result of being born
again is a belief that Jesus is the Christ. Of course,
this faith that comes from the new birth is a real
faith. The faith that John spoke of here is not a faith
that is a mere opinion, but a real faith that Jesus is
the anointed of God—a faith that leads us to en-
throne Jesus as King in our lives. If you are not
making Jesus the King of your heart and life, you
have not been born again. But if you are making Jesus the King of your heart and life, and absolute
Ruler of your thoughts and conduct, then you are
born again, for *"whoever believes that Jesus is the
Christ is born of God."*

We Have Victory over the World

We find the fifth result of being born again
three verses further down in this same chapter:
"For whatever is born of God overcomes the world"
(1 John 5:4). The fifth result of being born of God is
victory over the world.

The world is in conflict with God. *"The whole
world lies under the sway of the wicked one"* (1 John
5:19). It is under the dominion of the Evil One, ruled
by his ambitions and ideas. The world fights against
God in its economic life, social life, domestic life, and
in all the phases of intellectual and educational life.
It is constantly exercising a power over each of us, to
draw us into disobedience to God.

But the person who is born of God by the power of faith gets victory over the world (1 John 5:4). He gets victory over the world's ideas, purposes, plans, and ambitions. Every day, he gets victory over the world in his personal life, domestic life, economic life, political life, and intellectual life.

We Do Not Make a Practice of Sin

The sixth result of being born of God is found in 1 John 3:9:

> *Whoever has been born of God does not sin, for His* [God's] *seed remains in him; and he cannot sin* [more literally, cannot be sinning], *because he has been born of God.*

The sixth result, then, in the one who is born of God is that the seed of God remains in him. Therefore, the one born of God is not making a practice of sin. Some people ask, Just what does this mean? It means exactly what it says if we look carefully at the exact definitions of the words and give due emphasis to the tense of the verbs.

First of all, let us look at the exact meaning of the word translated *"sin."* What does *"sin"* mean? John himself was careful to define it in the verse itself and in the context in which our verse is found. The first thing that is evident from 1 John 3:9 is that *"sin"* is something that a person does, not merely something that he leaves undone, and not merely sinful thoughts and desires. What kind of "something" is defined five verses back in verse 4: *"Whoever commits sin also commits lawlessness, and sin is lawlessness."* Here, by John's own definition (and we have no right to bring the definition of anyone else into the verse we are studying), *"sin is lawlessness."* That is, sins are acts that reveal conscious disregard for the will of God as revealed in His Word.

So we see that sin, as used here, means a conscious, intentional violation of the law of God. The regenerate individual will not be doing what he knows is contrary to the will of God. He may do what is contrary to God's will when he does not know it is contrary to God's will. In that case, his action is not, therefore, *"lawlessness."* Perhaps he ought to have known that it was contrary to God's will, and when he is led to see that it is, he will confess his guilt to God.

Furthermore, we should note the tense of the verb used in 1 John 3:9. It is the present tense, which denotes progressive or continuous action. A literal translation of the passage would be, "Whoever has been born of God is not doing sin, because His (God's) seed in him is remaining; and he cannot be sinning, because he has been born of God." It is not taught here that a born-again believer never sins in a single act, but it is taught that he is not going on sinning or making a practice of sin. We see what he is practicing in 1 John 2:29: *"If you know that He is righteous, you know that everyone who practices righteousness is born of Him."*

The result, then, in a born-again believer is that he does not go on consciously, day after day, doing what he knows is contrary to the will of God. But he does make a practice of "doing righteousness," that is, doing God's will as revealed in His Word. The new nature imparted in regeneration renders the continuous practice of sin impossible and renders the practice of righteousness inevitable.

We Love Our Fellow Believers

The seventh result of the new birth is found in 1 John 3:14: *"We know that we have passed from death to life, because we love the brethren. He who does not love his brother abides in death."* The seventh result of being born again is that we love our brothers and sisters in Christ. We should note carefully what the meaning of *"love"* is as brought out in the context. It is not love as a mere sentiment. It is love in that higher and deeper sense of a desire for and delight in the welfare of others, the sort of love that leads us to make sacrifices for those we love. As we read further down in this same chapter,

> *By this we know love, because He laid down His life for us. And we also ought to lay down our lives for the brethren. But whoever has this world's goods, and sees his brother in need, and shuts up his heart from him, how does the love of God abide in him? My little children, let us not love in word or in tongue, but in deed and in truth.* (1 John 3:16–18)

This passage makes it very evident that what the Holy Spirit means by *"love"* here is not a mere affection or fondness for others, not a mere delight in their company. It means a deep and genuine interest in their welfare that leads us to dig into our pockets when they are in need and supply their need. It leads us to sacrifice our own interests for the sake of their interests, even to the point of laying down our lives for them.

The objects of this love are *"the brethren,"* that is, all those who are born of God. We read in 1 John 5:1: *"Whoever believes that Jesus is the Christ is born of God, and everyone who loves Him who begot also loves him who is begotten of Him."* Any person who is born again will love every other person who is born again. The other individual may be an American, a German, an Englishman, an African-American, or an Indian; the individual may be educated or uneducated; but the person is a child of God and a brother or a sister. As such, he or she will be the object of your love if you are born of God. This is a searching test of whether or not a person is born again.

We Are New

The final result that we will consider is found in 2 Corinthians 5:17: *"Therefore, if anyone is in Christ, he is a new creation; old things have passed away; behold, all things have become new."* The eighth result of being born again is that in the regenerate person, *"old things have passed away"* and *"all things have become new."* In the place of the old ideas, old desires, old purposes, and old choices are new ideas, new desires, new purposes, and new choices.

Why Is It Necessary to Be Born Again?

For just a few paragraphs, let us look at the necessity of the new birth. This is set forth in the following verses:

> *Most assuredly, I say to you, unless one is born of water and the Spirit, he cannot enter the kingdom of God. That which is born of the flesh is flesh, and that which is born of the Spirit is spirit.*   *(John 3:5–6)*

We see here that the new birth is a universal necessity, and we see why it is a universal necessity. Verse 6 tells us that all that one gets by natural birth is *"flesh,"* and the kingdom of God is spiritual. Therefore, to enter it, one must be *"born of the Spirit."*

No matter how refined and intelligent our ancestry is, no matter how godly our fathers and mothers may have been, we do not get the Holy Spirit from them. All we get is *"flesh."* It may be refined flesh, moral flesh, upright flesh, and very attractive flesh, but it is flesh. We know that *"those who are in the flesh cannot please God"* (Rom. 8:8) or *"inherit the kingdom of God"* (1 Cor. 15:50). We also know that the flesh is incapable of improvement. *"Can... the leopard* [change] *its spots?"* (Jer. 13:23). Of course not. Nor can a person who is unregenerate change his life in such a way that it will be pleasing to God. He must be born again.

The new birth is absolutely imperative, so imperative that Jesus said to Nicodemus—though he was a man of most exemplary morality, a man of high moral and spiritual education, a leader in Israel's religious life—*"You must be born again"* (John 3:7). Nothing else will take the place of the new birth. People are trying to substitute education, morality, religion, orthodoxy, baptism, outward reform, New Thought, Theosophy, the knowledge of God, and other such things; but none of these, nor all of them put together, are sufficient. You *must* be born again. There is absolutely no exception to this rule. As Jesus said in John 3:3, *"Most assuredly, I say to you, unless one is born again, he cannot see the kingdom of God."*

How Can a Person Be Born Again?

This question, therefore, confronts each one of us: Have you been born again? There is no more important question that you could possibly face. Face it in these pages, and don't dodge it.

This brings us to the immediately practical question: How are individuals born again? Or, What must anyone reading this who is not born again do in order to be born again right now? This question is plainly answered in the Word of God. I can answer it in very few paragraphs and in a way that anyone reading this can understand. There are three parts to the answer.

By God's Working

You will find the first part of the answer in Titus 3:5:

Not by works of righteousness which we have done, but according to His mercy He [God] saved us, through the washing of regeneration and renewing of the Holy Spirit.

These words tell us very plainly that it is God who regenerates and that He does it through the power of His Holy Spirit.

The same thought is found in John 3:5–6:

Jesus answered, "Most assuredly, I say to you, unless one is born of water and the Spirit, he cannot enter the kingdom of God. That which is born of the flesh is flesh, and that which is born of the Spirit is spirit."

Regeneration is God's work, performed by Him by the power of His Holy Spirit working in the mind, feelings, and will of the one born again—in your heart and mine.

By Getting in Contact with God's Word

Someone might infer from the fact that regeneration is God's work that all we have to do is wait until God sees fit to work. But we see plainly from other passages in the Word that this is not true. In James 1:18, we are taught the second thing concerning how regeneration is brought about: *"Of His own will He brought us forth by the word of truth, that we might be a kind of firstfruits of His creatures."* Here we are taught that the Word of Truth, the Word of God, is the instrument that God uses in regeneration.

The same thought is found in 1 Peter 1:23: *"Having been born again, not of corruptible seed but incorruptible, through the word of God which lives and abides forever."* And Paul gave voice to the same great thought in 1 Corinthians 4:15, where he said,

> *For though you might have ten thousand instructors in Christ, yet you do not have many fathers; for in Christ Jesus I have begotten you through the gospel.*

From these passages, it is evident that the new birth is brought about by God through the instrument of His Word. It is God who works through the power of His Holy Spirit, but the Holy Spirit works through the Word. Thus God makes individuals new by the Word of Truth, or the Word of God—that is, the Word that is preached by the Gospel. So then, if you or I wish to be born again, we should get in contact with the Word of God by studying the Bible and asking God that the Holy Spirit would make the Word that we are studying a living thing in our own hearts. We should get in contact especially with the gospel of John, for John told us in John 20:31,

> *These* [that is, these things in the gospel of John] *are written that you may believe that Jesus is the Christ, the Son of God, and that believing you may have life in His name.*

If we wish to see others born again, we should use the Word of God effectively to touch their minds and hearts, either by preaching the Word, teaching

the Word, or using the Word in our personal minis-
try. We should look to the Holy Spirit to make that
Word alive in the hearts of people as we sow it there.
In this way, the new birth will result.

By Trusting in Jesus

The third, last, and decisive truth as to how we
are born again is found in Galatians 3:26 and John
1:12–13. In Galatians 3:26, we read, *"For you are all
sons of God through faith in Christ Jesus."* This
verse tells us plainly that we become born again
through putting our faith in Christ Jesus. This is
even more explicitly stated in John 1:12–13:

> *But as many as received Him* [the Lord Jesus],
> *to them He gave the right to become children of
> God, to those who believe in His name: who
> were born, not of blood, nor of the will of the
> flesh, nor of the will of man, but of God.*

Here we are told that the decisive thing in our becoming children of God is that we believe in, or receive, Jesus Christ. We must (1) receive Jesus Christ
as our personal Savior and trust God to forgive us
because Jesus Christ died in our place, (2) receive
Him as our Lord and King and surrender our
thoughts and lives to His absolute control, and (3) be
willing to confess Jesus Christ as Lord before the
world. Anyone who does these things is immediately
a child of God, is immediately born again, is immediately made a partaker of the divine nature (2 Pet.
1:4).

The same thought was illustrated by Jesus Himself in John 3:14–15, where our Lord Jesus is recorded as saying,

> *And as Moses lifted up the serpent in the wilderness, even so must the Son of Man be lifted up, that whoever believes in Him should not perish but have eternal life.*

The reference is to the Old Testament story of how the Israelites were bitten by *"fiery serpents."* (See Numbers 21:4–9.) The dying Israelite, with the poison of the fiery serpent coursing through his veins, was saved by simply looking at the bronze serpent on the pole, a serpent that looked like the one that had bitten him. He had new life as soon as he looked. In the same way, we dying individuals, with the poison of sin coursing through our veins, are saved by looking at Jesus Christ, who was made *"in the likeness of sinful flesh"* (Rom. 8:3) and lifted up on the cross. We have new life the moment we look. The only part we have to play in our regeneration is to receive Christ as He is presented to us in the Word, by which we are born again. *"Therefore, if anyone is in Christ, he is a new creation; old things have passed away; behold, all things have become new"* (2 Cor. 5:17).

In the new birth, the Word of God is the seed, and the human heart is the soil. The preacher of the Word is the sower who drops the seed of the Word into the soil of the human heart. (See Luke 8:11–15.) God, by His Spirit, opens the heart to receive the seed (Acts 16:14). The hearer believes, and the Spirit gives life to the seed in the receptive heart. The heart closes around the seed by faith. The new nature, the divine nature, springs up out of the divine Word, and the believer is *"born again"* (1 Pet. 1:23), is *"made alive"* (Eph. 2:1), has *"passed out of death into life"* (1 John 3:14 RV).

You Can Be Born Again

Have you been born again? I ask this question of everyone reading this book. I do not ask whether you are a church member. I do not ask whether you have been baptized. I do not ask whether you have gone regularly to communion. I do not ask whether you have turned over a new leaf. I do not ask whether you are a likable, cultured, intelligent, moral, or popular person. I ask you, Have you been born again? If not, you are outside of the kingdom of God and are headed for an everlasting hell.

But you can be born again today. You can be born again before you put this book down. You can be born again right now, for the Word of God says,

> *But as many as received Him, to them He gave the right to become children of God, to those who believe in His name: who were born, not of blood, nor of the will of the flesh, nor of the will of man, but of God.*   *(John 1:12–13)*

And it says again in Romans 10:9–10,

> *If you confess with your mouth the Lord Jesus and believe in your heart that God has raised*

> *Him from the dead, you will be saved. For*
> *with the heart one believes unto righteousness,*
> *and with the mouth confession is made unto*
> *salvation.*

These verses make it as plain as day just what you must do right here and now to become a child of God. It is up to you to say whether or not you will do it.

Four

What Is Sanctification, and How Can It Be Mine?

What Is Sanctification, and How Can It Be Mine?

Now may the God of peace Himself
sanctify you completely; and may your whole spirit,
soul, and body be preserved blameless at the
coming of our Lord Jesus Christ.
—1 Thessalonians 5:23

The subject of sanctification is of great importance. Not only is there much ignorance and error and misconception about the subject, but there is also, strange to say, much bitter controversy over it. Some years ago, there were two rival "holiness conventions" held at the same time in Chicago at different hours of the day, in the same church. The animosity between these two groups of "holiness brethren" was so intense that on one occasion they came close to having a fistfight at the altar of the church.

The subject of sanctification has given rise to such bitterness and such extremes in some places that many even dread the use of the word. But *sanctification* is a Bible word and a deeply significant word, a word full of precious meaning. It would not be wise to give up this good Bible word simply because it is so often abused.

On one occasion, at the Bible Institute of Chicago, a man said to me, "Aren't you afraid of holiness?" Of course, what the man wanted to know was whether I was afraid of certain aspects of so-called holiness doctrine. I replied that I was not nearly as afraid of holiness as I was of unholiness.

The teaching of the Bible on this subject is very plain and very precious. What I have to say about it will come under three main questions: What is sanctification? How are we sanctified? When does sanctification take place?

What Is Sanctification?

Before we consider what sanctification is, it is important to see what sanctification is not. There are many things that it is not, but I would like to discuss two of them.

What Sanctification Is Not

In the first place, let me make it clear that sanctification is not the baptism with the Holy Spirit. These two experiences are constantly confused. There is an intimate relationship between the two, but they are not one and the same thing at all. Only confusion and misconception can arise when we combine two experiences that God keeps separate. Sanctification is not the baptism with the Holy Spirit, and the baptism with the Holy Spirit is not sanctification. This fact will become clear as we proceed.

In the second place, let me say that sanctification is not the eradication of the carnal nature. We will see this when we examine God's definition of sanctification, for God has very clearly defined what sanctification is and when it takes place. Those who teach the eradication of the carnal nature are grasping after a great and precious truth, but they have expressed that truth in a very inaccurate, unfortunate, and unscriptural way. Their way of stating it leads to grave misunderstandings, errors, and abuses.

The whole controversy about the eradication of the carnal nature comes from a misunderstanding, and from using terms for which there is no warrant in the Bible. The Bible nowhere speaks about "the carnal nature," and so it certainly does not speak about the eradication of the carnal nature. There is such a thing as a carnal nature, but it is not a material thing or substance. It is not something that can be eradicated in the same way that a doctor can pull a tooth or remove an appendix. A carnal nature is a nature controlled by the flesh (the sinful tendencies of man). Certainly, it is a believer's privilege not to have his nature governed by the flesh. His nature may be and should be under the control of the Holy Spirit, and then it is not a carnal nature. But one nature has not been eradicated and then replaced by another nature. The believer's nature is taken out from under the control of the flesh and put under the control of the Holy Spirit.

Furthermore, while it is the Christian's privilege to have his nature under the control of the Holy Spirit and to have it delivered from the control of the flesh, he still has the flesh, and he will have the

flesh as long as he is in this body. But if he *"walk*[s]
in the Spirit," he does not *"fulfill the lust of the
flesh"* (Gal. 5:16).

The eighth chapter of Romans describes the
life of victory, just as the seventh chapter, in verses
9–24, describes the life of defeat, the life of being
"carnal, sold under sin" (v. 14). It is in the eighth
chapter, where life *"in the Spirit"* (v. 9) is de-
scribed, that we are told that we still have the
flesh, but that it is our privilege not to *"live according to the flesh"* (v. 12) but to *"by the Spirit...put to
death the deeds of the body"* (v. 13). So we see that
the flesh is there, but in the power of the Spirit, we
do day by day (and if we live up to our privilege,
hour by hour and minute by minute) *"put to death
the deeds of the body."*

What Sanctification Is

That will suffice as an explanation of what sanctification is not. Now we will see exactly what it is by
looking at God's definition. The word *sanctification*
is used in the Bible in a twofold sense.

We find the first meaning of sanctification in
Leviticus 8:10–12:

> *Also Moses took the anointing oil, and
> anointed the tabernacle and all that was in it,
> and consecrated [*"sanctified"* KJV] them. He
> sprinkled some of it on the altar seven times,
> anointed the altar and all its utensils, and the
> laver and its base, to consecrate [*"sanctify"*
> KJV] them. And he poured some of the anoint-
> ing oil on Aaron's head and anointed him, to
> consecrate [*"sanctify"* KJV] him.*

Now, it is perfectly clear in this passage that *"sanctify"* means "to separate or set apart for God" and that sanctification is "the process of setting apart or the state of being set apart for God."

The word *sanctify* is used in this sense over and over again in the Bible. Another illustration is Leviticus 27:14, 16:

> *And when a man dedicates ["shall sanctify"* KJV] *his house to be holy to the LORD, then the priest shall set a value for it, whether it is good or bad; as the priest values it, so it shall stand....If a man dedicates ["shall sanctify"* KJV] *to the LORD part of a field of his possession, then your valuation shall be according to the seed for it.*

Still another instance of this same use of the word *sanctify* is found in Numbers 8:17:

> *For all the firstborn among the children of Israel are Mine, both man and beast; on the day that I struck all the firstborn in the land of Egypt I sanctified them to Myself.*

This verse, of course, does not mean that at the time that God smote the firstborn in Egypt, He eradicated the carnal nature from the firstborn of Israel. It does mean that He set apart all the firstborn to be uniquely His own.

Another very significant illustration of the same usage of the word is found in Jeremiah's statement of his own case:

> *Then the word of the LORD came to me, saying: "Before I formed you in the womb I knew*

*you; before you were born I sanctified you; I
ordained you a prophet to the nations."*

(Jer. 1:4–5)

This passage plainly means that before Jeremiah's
birth, God set him apart for Himself. There would
still be much imperfection and weakness in him, but
he was set apart for God.

Another thought-provoking instance of the same
use of the word *sanctify* is found in Matthew 23:17,
in the words of our Lord Jesus Himself: *"Fools and
blind! For which is greater, the gold or the temple
that sanctifies the gold?"* But perhaps the most
striking illustration of all is in what our Lord said
about His own sanctification in John 17:19: *"And for
their sakes I sanctify myself, that they themselves also
may be sanctified in truth"* (RV). Here the plain
meaning is that our Lord Jesus set Himself apart for
this work for God, and He did it in order that believers might be set apart for God *"in truth,"* or "in the
truth."

This is the most frequent use of the word *sanctify*. There are numerous illustrations of it in the Bible. So sanctify means "to separate or to set apart
for God," and sanctification is "the process of setting
apart or the state of being set apart for God." This is
the primary meaning of the words.

But sanctification, as used in the Bible, also has
a secondary definition closely related to this primary
meaning. We find an illustration of this secondary
definition in 2 Chronicles 29:5:

*Hear me, Levites! Now sanctify yourselves,
sanctify the house of the LORD God of your*

> *fathers, and carry out the rubbish from the*
> *holy place.*

When we bear in mind the parallelism that is the chief characteristic of Hebrew poetry, it is plain that to sanctify here is synonymous with "[to] *carry out the rubbish from the holy place."* So here, to sanctify means "to separate from ceremonial or moral defilement; to cleanse"; and sanctification is "the process of separating, or the state of being separated, from ceremonial or moral defilement."

The same use of the word is found in Leviticus 11:44:

> *For I am the LORD your God: ye shall therefore*
> *sanctify yourselves, and ye shall be holy; for I*
> *am holy: neither shall ye defile yourselves with*
> *any manner of creeping thing that creepeth*
> *upon the earth.*   *(KJV)*

Here again, it is clear that *"sanctify yourselves"* is synonymous with *"ye shall be holy"* and is contrasted with *"defile yourselves."*

The same meaning of sanctification is found in the New Testament in 1 Thessalonians 5:23:

> *Now may the God of peace Himself sanctify*
> *you completely; and may your whole spirit,*
> *soul, and body be preserved blameless at the*
> *coming of our Lord Jesus Christ.*

Here we see the close relationship between entire sanctification and being preserved wholly, without blame. To sanctify here clearly means "to separate from moral defilement," and sanctification, here again, is "the process of separating, or the state of being separated, from moral defilement."

The same thing is evident from 1 Thessalonians 4:7: *"For God called us not for uncleanness, but in sanctification"* (RV). Here our *"sanctification"* is set in direct contrast to *"uncleanness"*; hence, it is evident that here sanctification means "the state of being separated from all moral defilement." The same concept is clear from the third verse of this same chapter: *"For this is the will of God, your sanctification: that you should abstain from sexual immorality."* Here again, it is evident that sanctification means "separation from impurity or moral defilement."

The two meanings, then, of sanctification are as follows: first, "the process of separating or setting apart, or the state of being separated or set apart, for God"; and second, "the process of separating, or the state of being separated, from ceremonial or moral defilement." These two meanings of the word are closely allied. One cannot be truly separated unto God without being separated from sin.

How Are We Sanctified?

We now come to the second question: How are we sanctified? There are several parts to the complete answer to this question.

God Sanctifies Us

The first part of the answer is found in the text of this chapter:

> *Now may the God of peace Himself sanctify*
> *you completely; and may your whole spirit,*
> *soul, and body be preserved blameless at the*
> *coming of our Lord Jesus Christ.*
>
> > *(1 Thess. 5:23)*

It appears from this verse that God sanctifies us, that sanctification is God's work. Both our separation from sin and our separation unto God is God's work. As it was God who in the Old Testament set apart the firstborn of Israel unto Himself, so it is God who in the New Testament sets apart the believer unto Himself and separates him from sin. Sanctification primarily is not ours, but God's.

Christ Sanctifies Us

The second part of the answer is found in Ephesians 5:25–26:

> *Husbands, love your wives, just as Christ also*
> *loved the church and gave Himself for her,*
> *that He might sanctify and cleanse her with*
> *the washing of water by the word.*

Here we are taught that Christ sanctifies the church and that sanctification is Christ's work. Of course, we are faced with the question, In what sense does Christ sanctify the church? The answer is found in Hebrews 10:10: *"By that will we have been sanctified through the offering of the body of Jesus Christ once for all."* Here it appears that Jesus Christ sanctified the church by giving Himself up as a sacrifice for it. In this way, Christ set the church apart for God.

Just as the blood of the Passover lamb, referred to in the eleventh and twelfth chapters of Exodus, made a difference between Israel and Egypt (Exod. 11:7), so our Lord Jesus, by the offering of His own body, has forever made a difference between the believer and the world. He has forever set every believer apart for God. The Cross of Christ stands between the believer and the world, and the shed blood of Christ separates the believer from the world and purchases him for God, thus making him belong to God.

The Holy Spirit Sanctifies Us

The third part of the answer to the question of how we are sanctified is found in 2 Thessalonians 2:13:

> *But we are bound to give thanks to God always for you, brethren beloved by the Lord, because God from the beginning chose you for salvation through sanctification by the Spirit and belief in the truth.*

It appears from this passage, as well as from other passages in the Bible, that it is the Holy Spirit who sanctifies the believer. Sanctification is the Holy Spirit's work.

Here the question arises, In what sense does the Holy Spirit sanctify the believer? Just as, in the Old Testament, tabernacle, altar, and priest were set apart for God by the anointing oil (Lev. 8:10–12), so in the New Testament, the believer, who is both tabernacle and priest, is set apart for God by the anointing of the Holy Spirit. Furthermore, it is the

Holy Spirit's work in the heart that overcomes the flesh and its defilement, and thus separates the believer from sin and clothes him with divine graces of character and makes him fit to be God's own.

As Paul put it in Galatians 5:22–23, *"The fruit of the Spirit is love, joy, peace, longsuffering, kindness, goodness, faithfulness, gentleness, self-control."* In direct contrast to this work of the Holy Spirit, we read in the immediately preceding verses about *"the works of the flesh"* (v. 19), an awful catalog of vileness and sin. However, we are told in the sixteenth verse, *"Walk in the Spirit, and you shall not fulfill the lust of the flesh."*

The Blood of Jesus Sanctifies Us

The fourth part of the answer to the question of how we are sanctified is found in Hebrews 13:12: *"Therefore Jesus also, that He might sanctify the people with His own blood, suffered outside the gate."* It is plain from this passage that believers are sanctified through the blood of Jesus Christ. But in what sense does the blood of Jesus sanctify? The answer is plain: the blood of Jesus Christ cleanses us from all the guilt of sin, and thus it separates us from all the people who are under the curse of the broken law and sets us apart for God. (See 1 John 1:7, 9.) In the Old Testament, the blood of the sacrifice cleansed the Israelites from the guilt of ceremonial offenses and set them apart for God. In the New Testament fulfillment of this Old Testament type, the blood of Christ cleanses the believer from the guilt of moral offenses and sets him apart for God.

The Word of God Sanctifies Us

The fifth part of the answer to the question of how we are sanctified is found in John 17:17: *"Sanctify them by Your truth. Your word is truth."* Here in our Lord Jesus' prayer, He indicated that we are sanctified by the truth and that the Word of God is the truth. In what sense does the Word of God sanctify us? This question is plainly answered in different parts of the Bible, where we are taught that the Word of God cleanses us from the presence of sin and thus separates us from it and sets us apart unto God. (See Psalm 119:9, 11; John 15:3.) As we bring our lives into daily contact with the Word, the sins and imperfections of our lives and hearts are disclosed and put away, and thus we are more and more separated from sin unto God. (See John 13:10.)

Taking Hold of Christ Sanctifies Us

The sixth part of the answer is found in 1 Corinthians 1:30: *"But of Him you are in Christ Jesus, who became for us wisdom from God; and righteousness and sanctification and redemption."* In this passage, we are taught that Jesus Christ became for us sanctification from God. Just what does this mean? Simply this: separation from sin and separation unto God are provided for us in Christ Jesus. By taking hold of Jesus Christ, we obtain this sanctification that has been provided. The more completely we take hold of Christ, the more completely we are sanctified. Perfect sanctification is provided for us in Him, just as perfect wisdom is provided for us in Him (Col. 2:3). We take hold of wisdom, sanctification, or anything else that is provided for us in Christ, in ever increasing measure. Through the indwelling Christ presented to us by the Spirit in the Word, we are made Christlike, and we bear fruit.

Our Pursuit of Holiness Sanctifies Us

The seventh part of the answer to the question of how we are sanctified is found in Hebrews 12:14: *"Follow after peace with all men, and the sanctification without which no man shall see the Lord"* (RV). Here we are taught that we have our own part in sanctification. If we are to be sanctified in the fullest sense, sanctification is something that we must pursue, or seek earnestly. While sanctification is God's work, we have our part in it, namely, to make it the object of our earnest desire and eager pursuit.

Presenting Ourselves to God Sanctifies Us

The eighth part of the answer is found in Romans 6:19, 22:

> *As ye presented your members as servants to uncleanness and to iniquity unto iniquity, even so now present your members as servants to righteousness unto sanctification....But now being made free from sin, and become servants to God, ye have your fruit unto sanctification.* (RV)

The meaning of these words is plain, and the teaching is important and practical. We are taught here that we attain to sanctification through presenting our members as servants (bondservants or slaves) to righteousness. In other words, if we want to attain to sanctification, we should present our whole bodies and every member of them to God to be His servants, belonging wholly to Him. We should present our whole selves to God as His servants, to be His property entirely. This is the practical method of attaining to sanctification, a method that is available to each one of us, no matter how weak we are in ourselves.

Faith in Christ Sanctifies Us

The ninth and final part of the answer to the question of how we are sanctified is found in Acts 26:18, where Jesus said,

> To open their eyes, in order to turn them from darkness to light, and from the power of Satan to God, that they may receive forgiveness of sins and an inheritance among those who are sanctified by faith in Me.

Here we are told that we are sanctified by faith in Christ. Sanctification—just like justification, regeneration, and adoption—is dependent on faith. Faith is the hand by which we take hold of the blessing of sanctification that God has provided for us through His Son's death on the cross, and through the Holy Spirit's power working in us. We claim sanctification by simple faith in the One who shed His blood and by surrendering ourselves to the control of the Holy Spirit, whom Jesus Christ gives.

When Does Sanctification Take Place?

We now come to the question about which there has been the most discussion, the most differences of opinion, the most controversy: When does sanctification take place? If we go to our Bibles to get the answer to this question, there does not need to be any difference of opinion. The answer has three parts.

The Moment We Believe

First, we find part of the answer in 1 Corinthians 1:2:

> *To the church of God which is at Corinth, to those who are sanctified in Christ Jesus, called to be saints, with all who in every place call on the name of Jesus Christ our Lord, both theirs and ours.*

Here the Holy Spirit, speaking through the apostle Paul, plainly declared that all the members of the church of God are already sanctified in Christ Jesus. Sanctification in this sense is not something that we are to look for in the future; it is something that has already taken place. The moment anyone becomes a member of the church of God by simple faith in Christ Jesus (for all who have faith in Christ Jesus are members of the church of God), in that moment, the person is sanctified. Every saved man, woman, and child, everyone who has a living faith in Jesus Christ, is sanctified.

In other words, our sanctification is involved in our salvation. But in what sense are all believers already sanctified? The answer to this question is found in Hebrews 10:10, 14:

> *By which will we have been sanctified through the offering of the body of Jesus Christ once for*

*all....For by one offering he hath perfected for
ever them that are sanctified.* (RV)

The meaning of this is plain. By *"the offering of the
body of Jesus Christ once for all"* on the cross of Calvary as a perfect atonement for sin, every believer is
cleansed forever from the guilt of sin. We are
"perfected for ever" as far as our standing before God
is concerned, and we are set apart for God. The sacrifice of Christ does not need to be repeated as the
Jewish sacrifices were (Heb. 10:1, 11). The work was
done *"once for all"* (v. 10); sin is put away, and put
away forever. (See Hebrews 9:26.) We are set apart
forever as God's special and eternal possession.

If you are a believer in Jesus Christ—that is, if
you have a living faith in Jesus Christ—you have a
right to say, "I am sanctified." Every believer in
Christ is a saint—not a saint in the sense that the
word is often used these days, but in the biblical
sense, as being set apart for God, belonging to God,
and being God's special property.

But there is another sense in which every believer may be fully sanctified today. This is found in
Romans 12:1:

*I beseech you therefore, brethren, by the mer-
cies of God, that you present your bodies a living sacrifice, holy, acceptable to God, which is
your reasonable service.*

In this passage, we see that it is the believer's present and blessed privilege, as well as his important
and solemn duty, to present his body to God as *"a
living sacrifice"*—not some part or parts of his body,

but his whole body with its every member and every ability. When we do present our whole bodies to God as living sacrifices, then we are wholly sanctified. Such an offering is well-pleasing to God. In the Old Testament, God sometimes showed His pleasure in an offering by sending down fire to take it to Himself. (See 1 Kings 18:36–39.) Likewise, when the whole body is thus offered to God, He will send down fire again, the fire of the Holy Spirit, and take to Himself what is presented.

The moment a believer presents himself as a living sacrifice to God, then, as far as his will—the governing purpose of his life, the very center of his being—is concerned, he is wholly God's, or "perfectly sanctified." He may and will still daily discover, as he studies the Word of God and is enlightened by the Holy Spirit, aspects of his life that are not in conformity with this new central purpose of his will. These habits, feelings, words, and actions must be confessed to God as blameworthy and must be put away. These areas of the believer's being and life must be brought, by God's Spirit and the indwelling Christ, into conformity with God's will as revealed in His Word.

The victory in this newly discovered and unclaimed territory may be instantaneous. For example, I may discover in myself an irritability that is clearly displeasing to God. I can go to God, confess it, renounce it, and then instantly—not by my own strength but by looking to Jesus and claiming His patience and gentleness—overcome it and never have another failure in that area. So it is with every other sin and weakness in my life that I am brought to see is displeasing to God.

As We Progress in Our Walk with God

But this is not the whole answer to the question of when we are sanctified. The second part of the answer is found in the following passages:

May the Lord make you increase and abound in love to one another and to all, just as we do to you. (1 Thess. 3:12)

Finally then, brethren, we urge and exhort in the Lord Jesus that you should abound more and more, just as you received from us how you ought to walk and to please God....Indeed you do so toward all the brethren who are in all Macedonia. But we urge you, brethren, that you increase more and more. (1 Thess. 4:1, 10)

Grow in the grace and knowledge of our Lord and Savior Jesus Christ. (2 Pet. 3:18)

But we all, with unveiled face, beholding as in a mirror the glory of the Lord, are being transformed into the same image from glory to glory, just as by the Spirit of the Lord. (2 Cor. 3:18)

But, speaking the truth in love, [we] may grow up in all things into Him who is the head; Christ; from whom the whole body, joined and knit together by what every joint supplies, according to the effective working by which every part does its share, causes growth of the body for the edifying of itself in love. (Eph. 4:15–16)

From these passages, we see that there is a progressive work of sanctification—an increasing in love; an abounding more and more in a godly walk and in pleasing God; a growing in the grace and the knowledge of our Lord and Savior Jesus Christ; a being transformed into the image of our Lord from glory to glory, each new gaze at Him making us more like Him; a growing up into Christ in all things, until we attain to a full-grown man, *"to the measure of the stature of the fullness of Christ"* (Eph. 4:13).

At the Coming of Our Lord Jesus Christ

Even yet, we have not found the whole answer to the question of when we are sanctified. We find the remainder of the answer in our text:

> *Now may the God of peace Himself sanctify you completely; and may your whole spirit, soul, and body be preserved blameless at the coming of our Lord Jesus Christ.*
> *(1 Thess. 5:23)*

Here we are plainly told that the complete sanctification of believers, complete in the fullest sense, is something that is to be sought in prayer and that is to be accomplished by God in the future and perfected at the coming of our Lord Jesus Christ.

The same thought is found again in 1 Thessalonians:

> *And may the Lord make you increase and abound in love to one another and to all, just*

> *as we do to you, so that He may establish your*
> *hearts blameless in holiness before our God*
> *and Father at the coming of our Lord Jesus*
> *Christ with all His saints.   (1 Thess. 3:12–13)*

It is *"at the coming of our Lord Jesus Christ with all His saints"* that He is to establish our hearts *"blameless in holiness before our God and Father."* It is at Christ's coming that our whole spirits and souls and bodies are to be preserved without blame.

The same thought is found in 1 John 3:2:

> *Beloved, now we are children of God; and it*
> *has not yet been revealed what we shall be, but*
> *we know that when He is revealed, we shall be*
> *like Him, for we shall see Him as He is.*

It is not in the life that now is, and it is not at death, that we are entirely sanctified, spirit, soul, and body. It is at the coming of our Lord Jesus Christ. This fact is one of the many reasons that the well-instructed believer constantly cries, *"Even so, come, Lord Jesus!"* (Rev. 22:20). Moreover, he cries, "Come quickly!"

Five

What Will My Resurrected Body Be Like?

What Will My Resurrected Body Be Like?

Remember that Jesus Christ, of the seed of David,
was raised from the dead according to my gospel.
—2 Timothy 2:8

For I delivered to you first of all that which I
also received: that Christ died for our sins according
to the Scriptures, and that He was buried,
and that He rose again the third day
according to the Scriptures.
—1 Corinthians 15:3–4

The resurrection of Christ was a resurrection of the body of Christ. What appeared to the disciples on the first resurrection day was not merely the indwelling Spirit of Jesus Christ, clothed with a new and entirely different body. Appearing before their eyes was the body that had been buried and raised again.

For us, this truth involves not merely the immortality of our own souls, but also the resurrection and eternal existence of our own bodies. Yet many people who say that they are doctrinally sound, Bible-believing Christians and believe in the immortality of the soul, do not believe in the resurrection of the body. In this chapter, we will examine what the Bible has to say about bodily resurrection.

The Fact of the Resurrection

First, we will consider the fact of the resurrection of the body of Jesus Christ and of our bodies.

Second Timothy 2:8, one of the texts of this chapter, says, *"Remember that Jesus Christ, of the seed of David, was raised from the dead according to my gospel."* Here Paul explicitly declared that Jesus Christ was raised from the dead according to the gospel that he preached. Now, what was raised? Certainly not Christ's soul. That did not die. Turning to Acts 2:25, 27–32, we find that the soul of the Lord Jesus went into hades, the abode of the dead. These are Peter's words, spoken on the Day of Pentecost:

> *For David says concerning Him* [Jesus]: *"...For You* [God] *will not leave my* [Jesus'] *soul in Hades, nor will You allow Your Holy One to see corruption* [that is, to undergo bodily corruption]. *You have made known to me the ways of life; You will make me full of joy in Your presence." Men and brethren, let me speak freely to you of the patriarch David, that he is both dead and buried, and his tomb is with us to this day. Therefore, being a prophet, and knowing that God had sworn with an oath to him that of the fruit of his body, according to the flesh, He would raise up the Christ to sit on his throne, he, foreseeing this,*

*spoke concerning the resurrection of the
Christ, that His soul was not left in Hades, nor
did His flesh see corruption. This Jesus God
has raised up, of which we are all witnesses.*

Here Peter declared that the soul of Jesus went to
hades and that it was *"His flesh,"* that is, His body,
that was kept from corruption and afterward raised.

Turning now to 1 Corinthians 15:3–4, the other
text of this chapter, we read these words of Paul:

*For I delivered to you first of all that which I
also received: that Christ died for our sins according to the Scriptures, and that He was
buried, and that He rose again the third day
according to the Scriptures.*

Here Paul declared that Jesus Christ *"died"* and *"was
buried"* and *"rose again."* What was raised? Paul
said that what was buried was raised. But what was
buried? Not the soul of the Lord Jesus, but His body.

Peter made this even plainer, if possible, in
1 Peter 3:18–20:

*Christ also suffered for sins once, the right-
eous for the unrighteous, that he might bring
us to God; being put to death in the flesh, but
quickened in the spirit; in which also he went
and preached unto the spirits in prison, which
aforetime were disobedient, when the longsuffering of God waited in the days of Noah. (RV)*

These words clearly mean that it was the body of
Jesus that was put to death, but that the spirit still

lived and went into hades. So it was the body that was raised; and the spirit, which had not died or become unconscious, came back to the body.

First Corinthians 15:12–19 removes all possibility of doubt on this point—that is, for anyone who goes to the Bible to find out what it actually teaches, not merely to see how he can twist and distort it to fit into his own preconceived opinions. Paul's Spirit-given words are:

> *Now if Christ is preached that He has been raised from the dead, how do some among you say that there is no resurrection of the dead?* [Notice, he does not say "no immortality of the soul," but *"no resurrection of the dead."*] *But if there is no resurrection of the dead, then Christ is not risen. And if Christ is not risen, then our preaching is empty and your faith is also empty. Yes, and we are found false witnesses of God, because we have testified of God that He raised up Christ, whom He did not raise up; if in fact the dead do not rise. For if the dead do not rise, then Christ is not risen. And if Christ is not risen, your faith is futile; you are still in your sins! Then also those who have fallen asleep in Christ have perished. If in this life only we have hope in Christ, we are of all men the most pitiable.*

There is no honest mistaking the plain meaning of these words. By the *"resurrection of the dead,"* Paul plainly meant a resurrection of the body. In the whole chapter, beyond a doubt, he is not talking about the immortality of the soul, but the resurrection of the body. The whole argument hinges on that fact. Here Paul clearly said that if the body of Jesus was not raised, then Christianity is a sham, our faith is in vain, and we Christians are to be pitied more than all other people. For if the body of Jesus was not raised, and if our bodies are not to be raised, then we Christians are making tremendous sacrifices for a lie. Paul further said that if our bodies are not to be raised, then Christ's body has not been raised, and Christianity is a fraud.

Christianity, as it is taught in the New Testament, stands or falls with the resurrection of the body of Jesus and the resurrection of our bodies. There is no room in Paul's argument for Charles Taze Russell's doctrine.* Russell taught that the resurrection of Jesus Christ was not a resurrection of the body that was crucified and laid in the grave. He said that the body of Jesus Christ was carried away and preserved somewhere, or else dissolved into gases. But Paul said here that if the body that was laid in the sepulcher was not raised, *"then our preaching is empty and your faith is also empty."*

In Luke 24:5–6, the angels at Jesus' tomb are recorded as saying to the women who came there, *"Why do you seek the living among the dead? He is not here, but is risen!"* Now, what were the women seeking? They were seeking the body of Jesus to embalm it. The angels said that what they were seeking was not there but was risen.

Furthermore, in the second part of verse 6 and in verse 7, the angels said,

---

* Charles Taze Russell was the founder of the Jehovah's Witnesses.

> *Remember how He spoke to you when He was still in Galilee, saying, "The Son of Man must be delivered into the hands of sinful men, and be crucified, and the third day rise again."*

Here they plainly told the women that what was crucified, which of course was the body of Jesus, had been raised. If the actual, literal body of Jesus had not been raised, these angels were liars.

These verses are only a few of the many passages that contain the clear-cut teaching that the very body of Jesus was raised from the dead. Either this teaching is true, and it is also true that our bodies will be raised from the dead, or Christianity is a lie from start to finish. But Christ was raised from the dead, and we will be raised. Or, as Paul put it in 1 Corinthians 15:20, *"Christ is risen from the dead, and has become the firstfruits of those who have fallen asleep."* The resurrection of our bodies will be the harvest that follows the resurrection of Christ's body, which was *"the firstfruits."*

The Characteristics of Our Resurrection Bodies

Since we have clearly settled the fact of the resurrection of the body of Jesus Christ and of our bodies, next we will consider the characteristics of our resurrection bodies.

Different from Our Earthly Bodies

First of all, we know that the body that is raised will not be identical to the body that was laid in the grave. This is apparent from 1 Corinthians 15:35–38:

But someone will say, "How are the dead raised up? And with what body do they come?" Foolish one, what you sow is not made alive unless it dies. And what you sow, you do not sow that body that shall be, but mere grain; perhaps wheat or some other grain. But God gives it a body as He pleases, and to each seed its own body.

Here we are told that when our bodies are raised, they will not be exactly the same as when they were buried, any more than the wheat that springs up is the same as the seed that was planted. However, just as the wheat comes from the seed and bears the most intimate relationship to it, so our resurrection bodies will come from the bodies that are buried and bear the most intimate relationship to them. The resurrection body will be the outcome of the body that is buried. It will be the old body made alive and transformed; or, as Paul put it in Philippians 3:20–21,

Jesus Christ...will transform our lowly body that it may be conformed to His glorious body, according to the working by which He is able even to subdue all things to Himself.

Similar to Christ's Glorified Body

The next thing that the Bible teaches about our resurrection bodies is that they will be like the glorified body of Jesus Christ. This fact is apparent from the verses just quoted, Philippians 3:20–21. Let us read them again:

Jesus Christ...will transform our lowly body that it may be conformed to His glorious body, according to the working by which He is able even to subdue all things to Himself.

Christ's resurrection body was not the same body that was laid in the sepulcher. It was the old body transformed and delivered from the limitations that He had while living here among men. It had new qualities imparted to it. Our bodies will also be transformed to be like this glorious body of Christ and will thus be delivered from the limitations to which they are subjected now. They will have new qualities imparted to them. The resurrected body will be a transformed body.

The character of its transformation is indicated by the transformation that took place in the body of Jesus Christ. A hint as to what that transformed body of Jesus Christ is like is found in that preview of His resurrection that was seen by Peter, James, and John on the Mount of Transfiguration. In Matthew's description of the appearance of Jesus at His transfiguration, he told us that *"His face shone like the sun, and His clothes became as white as the light"* (Matt. 17:2). Luke told us that *"the appearance of His face was altered, and His robe became white and glistening"* (Luke 9:29). Mark told us that *"He was transfigured before them. His clothes became shining, exceedingly white, like snow, such as no launderer on earth can whiten them"* (Mark 9:2–3).

Not Composed of Flesh and Blood

The next thing that we are told about our resurrection bodies is that they will not be flesh and blood. In 1 Corinthians 15:50–51, we read, *"Now this I say, brethren, that flesh and blood cannot inherit the kingdom of God."* Here Paul was talking about our resurrection bodies. It is in the resurrection chapter that he said this, and he distinctly told us that our resurrection bodies will not be *"flesh and blood."*

Composed of Flesh and Bones

But while our resurrection bodies will not be flesh and blood, they will have flesh and bones. This is apparent from what our Lord Himself said about His own resurrection body in Luke 24:39: *"Behold My hands and My feet, that it is I Myself. Handle Me and see, for a spirit does not have flesh and bones as you see I have."* Since our bodies are to be transformed to be like His, our resurrection bodies will have *"flesh and bones."* Some have objected that there is a contradiction between what our Lord said here and what Paul said in the passage quoted above (1 Cor. 15:50–51), but there is no contradiction. *"Flesh"* we will have, but not *"flesh and blood,"* that is, not the flesh that has blood as its animating principle.

So we are faced with the question, What will take the place of blood in our resurrection bodies? The answer seems to be that in our present existence, *"blood is the life"* (Deut. 12:23) of the natural body; but in our future existence, our bodies are to be, as we are told in 1 Corinthians 15:44, *"spiritual"* bodies. That is, our bodies will have the Spirit of God as their animating principle, not their own blood. Although I cannot delve into the specifics of this truth, let me just say that our not having blood in our resurrection bodies involves many great and glorious possibilities.

Not Subject to Corruption

The fifth point, which is closely connected with the third and fourth points, is that our resurrection bodies will be incorruptible. We read in 1 Corinthians 15:42, *"So also is the resurrection of the dead. The body is sown in corruption, it is raised in incorruption."* The idea behind this word *"incorruption"* is that the body is not subject to decay; it is imperishable. Our present bodies are decaying all the time. We are perishing every day and every minute. My present body is disintegrating even as I write this chapter. But the bodies that we will receive in the resurrection will be absolutely free from corruption or decay. They *cannot* disintegrate or suffer decay or deterioration of any kind.

Glorious in Beauty

The next thing that we are taught about the resurrection body is that it is a glorious body. This comes out in the following verse: *"It is sown in dishonor, it is raised in glory"* (1 Cor. 15:43). We have some idea of the glory, the glorious beauty, of that body from the description of our glorified Lord in Revelation 1:13–17:

> *And in the midst of the seven lampstands One like the Son of Man, clothed with a garment down to the feet and girded about the chest*

with a golden band. His head and hair were white like wool, as white as snow, and His eyes like a flame of fire; His feet were like fine brass, as if refined in a furnace, and His voice as the sound of many waters; He had in His right hand seven stars, out of His mouth went a sharp two-edged sword, and His countenance was like the sun shining in its strength. And when I saw Him, I fell at His feet as dead. But He laid His right hand on me, saying to me, "Do not be afraid; I am the First and the Last."

Our resurrection bodies will be like that.

Complete and Powerful

Furthermore, the resurrection body will be powerful; or, as we read in the last half of 1 Corinthians 15:43, *"It is sown in weakness, it is raised in power."* Then all our weariness and weakness will be forever at an end. Our present bodies are often a hindrance to our highest aspirations. They thwart the carrying out of our loftiest purposes. *"The spirit indeed is willing, but the flesh is weak"* (Matt. 26:41). But the resurrection body will be able to accomplish all that the spirit purposes. The redeemed body will be a perfect counterpart of the redeemed spirit that inhabits it. There will be no deafness, nearsightedness, or blindness; no tired hands and feet; no lameness or missing limbs.

Heavenly in Nature

The resurrection body will be a heavenly body. This truth is apparent from 1 Corinthians 15:47–49:

The first man was of [literally, "out of"] *the
earth, made of dust; the second Man is the
Lord from* [literally, "out of"] *heaven. As was
the man of dust, so also are those who are
made of dust; and as is the heavenly Man, so
also are those who are heavenly. And as we
have borne the image of the man of dust, we
shall also bear the image of the heavenly Man.*

The thought plainly is that our present bodies are of
an earthly origin and an earthly character, but that
our transformed bodies will be of a heavenly origin
and a heavenly character. Paul explained this at
length in 2 Corinthians 5:1–4, where he said,

*For we know that if our earthly house, this
tent, is destroyed, we have a building from
God, a house not made with hands, eternal in
the heavens. For in this* [in these present
earthly houses, or earthy bodies] *we groan,
earnestly desiring to be clothed with our habitation which is from heaven* [that is, our heavenly bodies], *if indeed, having been clothed, we
shall not be found naked. For we who are in
this tent* [in these present earthy bodies]
*groan, being burdened, not because we want to
be unclothed, but further clothed* [that is, with
our heavenly bodies], *that mortality may be
swallowed up by life.*

Bright and Shining

Our transformed bodies will be luminous, shining, dazzling, bright like the sun. This fact is seen in
many passages. Take, for example, Matthew 13:43:

"Then the righteous will shine forth as the sun in the kingdom of their Father." This sentence is to be taken literally, for it is in the *interpretation* of one of the parables found in this chapter, not in the parable itself. This verse suggests what we have already seen about the transfigured body of Jesus in Matthew 17:2, where we are told that *"His face shone like the sun, and His clothes became as white as the light."*

We also have the same thought in the Old Testament in Daniel 12:3, where we are told, *"Those who are wise shall shine like the brightness of the firmament, and those who turn many to righteousness like the stars forever and ever."* They will shine literally as well as figuratively.

A hint of the luminous glory of our resurrection bodies is revealed in the light that Paul saw beaming from the person of Jesus Christ. In Paul's description of his encounter with the glorified Jesus on the Damascus road, we read,

> As I journeyed to Damascus with authority and commission from the chief priests, at midday, O king, along the road I saw a light from heaven, brighter than the sun, shining around me and those who journeyed with me.
> *(Acts 26:12–13)*

The light that Paul saw, as is evident from the whole account, was the light that shone from the person of our glorified Lord. In our resurrection bodies, we will be like Him.

Like the Angels

Three interesting facts regarding our resurrection bodies are stated in Matthew 22:30 and Luke

20:35–36. In Matthew 22:30, we read, *"For in the resurrection they neither marry nor are given in marriage, but are like angels of God in heaven."* In Luke 20:35–36, we read,

> But those who are counted worthy to attain that age, and the resurrection from the dead, neither marry nor are given in marriage; nor can they die anymore, for they are equal to the angels and are sons of God, being sons of the resurrection.

Taking these two passages together, we learn that in our resurrected state we will be like the angels, that in our resurrection bodies we will not marry, and that in our resurrection bodies we cannot die anymore.

Unique in Their Glory

Though all our resurrection bodies will be glorious, they will differ from one another, each one having its own particular glory. This is apparent from 1 Corinthians 15:41–42:

> There is one glory of the sun, another glory of the moon, and another glory of the stars; for one star differs from another star in glory. So also is the resurrection of the dead.

As glorious as all our bodies will be, there will be no tiresome uniformity, even of glory, in the world of resurrection bodies. Each body will have its own unique glory.

An Outward Manifestation of Our Sonship

In regard to the characteristics of our resurrection bodies, I would like to make one more point. The resurrection of our bodies will be the culmination of our adoption, that is, the completion of our being established as sons, or of our manifestation as sons of God. In Romans 8:23, we read,

> *We also who have the firstfruits of the Spirit, even we ourselves groan within ourselves, eagerly waiting for the adoption* [that is, our manifestation as sons], *the redemption of our body.*

When I say that the resurrection body will reveal the completion of our being established as sons, I mean that it will be outwardly manifested in the resurrection body that we are sons of God. Before His incarnation, Christ was *"in the form* [visible appearance] *of God"* (Phil. 2:6). So will we be also in the resurrection, for our bodies will be like His.

This truth sheds light on what Paul meant when he said in Colossians 3:4, *"When Christ, who is our life, shall be manifested, then shall ye also with him be manifested in glory"* (RV). It also sheds light on what John meant when he said in 1 John 3:2,

> *Beloved, now we are children of God; and it has not yet been revealed what we shall be, but we know that when He is revealed, we shall be like Him, for we shall see Him as He is.*

The Timing of the Resurrection of Our Bodies

There remains only one question to be considered in this chapter, and we can deal with it briefly.

This question is, When will the resurrection of the body take place? The Bible plainly answers this question time and time again. Read, for example, Philippians 3:20–21:

> *For our citizenship is in heaven, from which we also eagerly wait for the Savior, the Lord Jesus Christ, who will transform our lowly body that it may be conformed to His glorious body, according to the working by which He is able even to subdue all things to Himself.*

Here it is plainly declared that the transformation of our bodies into the likeness of Christ's glorious body will take place when the One whom we are awaiting appears from heaven. The same thought is given in 1 Thessalonians 4:16–17:

> *For the Lord Himself will descend from heaven with a shout, with the voice of an archangel, and with the trumpet of God. And the dead in Christ will rise first. Then we who are alive and remain shall be caught up together with them in the clouds to meet the Lord in the air. And thus we shall always be with the Lord.*

Perhaps you are wondering, What will happen to us in the meantime if we happen to die before the coming of the Lord? This question is also plainly answered:

> *For we know that if our earthly house, this tent* [our present bodies], *is destroyed* [dies and decays], *we have a building from God, a*

house not made with hands [our resurrection bodies that we are to receive at the coming of the Lord], *eternal in the heavens. For in this* [that is, while living in this present body] *we groan, earnestly desiring to be clothed with our habitation which is from heaven* [our resurrection bodies], *if indeed, having been clothed, we shall not be found naked. For we who are in this tent* [this present earthy body] *groan, being burdened, not because we want to be unclothed* [that is, not because we would merely like to get rid of our present bodies], *but further clothed* [that is, we want to receive our resurrection bodies], *that mortality may be swallowed up by life. Now He who has prepared us for this very thing is God, who also has given us the Spirit as a guarantee* [that is, the Holy Spirit, whom we have received as a deposit guaranteeing the full redemption in our resurrection bodies, which are to be obtained at the coming of the Lord]. *So we are always confident, knowing that while we are at home in the body* [that is, while we are still living our earthly lives in these present earthly bodies] *we are absent from the Lord. For we walk by faith, not by sight. We are confident, yes, well pleased rather to be absent from the body* [that is, to have our present earthly bodies die even before we get our resurrection bodies, which we will not receive until the return of the Lord] *and to be present with the Lord.*   *(2 Cor. 5:1–8)*

The plain teaching of this passage is that if we die before the return of the Lord and therefore before we obtain our resurrection bodies, our spirits will be unclothed, that is, they will be unclothed from these present bodies, and will not yet be clothed with our resurrection bodies. Nevertheless, we will be at home with the Lord in conscious blessedness—in a condition that is far better than that of this present life (see Philippians 1:23), but not as perfect as the condition that will exist when our redeemed spirits are clothed with our resurrection bodies. It will be at the return of the Lord Jesus that we will receive our full redemption. That is one reason that we *"eagerly wait for the Savior"* (Phil. 3:20).

There are many reasons that we long for the return of our Lord. All the great problems that are confronting us at this present time in national and international life, in social, economic, and political life, will be solved when He comes—and not until He comes. For this reason, we eagerly wait for Him. But we long for Him also because, while this present body serves many a useful purpose for the redeemed spirit that inhabits it, it is often a hindrance. The human body is often subject to aches, pains, and frailties, and it is constantly subject to temptations. But when our Lord Jesus comes again, He will transform these lowly bodies of ours into the likeness of His own glorious body (Phil. 3:21). At that time, we will know what "full salvation" means. Then we will shine forth like the sun in the kingdom of our Father (Matt. 13:43).

Six

How Can
I Defeat
the Devil?

How Can I Defeat the Devil?

The devil...is.
—John 8:44

The devil has sinned.
—1 John 3:8

The biblical doctrine concerning the Devil—his existence, nature, character, work, and destiny—is a fundamental doctrine of the Christian faith and is of vital importance. The teaching of the Bible on this subject is not a matter of mere theory or useless philosophy, but it is a matter of truths that have practical, everyday importance. Experience shows that if people are in error on this subject, they are pretty sure to be in error on other fundamental doctrines. When men and women begin to question the existence of a personal Devil—one that has the qualities of a person, such as a personality and a will—before long, they will likely challenge a good many other things that a true child of God should not question.

Doubt about the existence of a literal Devil is widespread today. The absolute denial of Satan's existence is one of the main points in Christian Science, a system that is doing much evil. Partly because of its denial of him, Christian Science has appropriately been called "The Devil's Masterpiece."

In addition, many supposedly sound preachers do not hesitate to say, "I do not believe in the existence of a real Devil." As I mentioned in the first chapter of this book, a well-known and popular pastor in Los Angeles proclaimed to his congregation that he was going to preach a gospel "without a Devil, without a hell, without an atonement of blood and retribution, without an infallible Bible." If he does omit any of these elements, he is preaching a system of doctrine that is different from what is contained in the Bible, which our Lord Jesus Christ has endorsed as the Word of God.

The Existence of the Devil

The first point I want to make clear is that there is a Devil. This fact is plain from our first text, John 8:44: *"The devil...is."* The verse in its entirety reads,

> *You are of your father the devil, and the desires of your father you want to do. He was a murderer from the beginning, and does not stand in the truth, because there is no truth in him. When he speaks a lie, he speaks from his own resources, for he is a liar and the father of it.*

These are the words of Jesus Christ. With anyone who has any right to call himself a Christian, the words of Jesus Christ have infinitely more weight than the words of Mary Baker Eddy or anyone else, or everyone else put together. Here Jesus said, *"The devil...is."*

By no means is this the only passage in which our Lord Jesus asserted in the most emphatic and unmistakable terms the existence of the Devil. We read these words in Matthew 13:19:

> *When anyone hears the word of the kingdom,*
> *and does not understand it, then the wicked*
> *one comes and snatches away what was sown*
> *in his heart.*

This verse is found in the interpretation of a parable—the parable of the sower. It is impossible to say that these words are figurative. In parables, we have symbolic language; in the explanation of the parables, we have the literal facts that the symbolic language represents. The words of Matthew 13:19 are not taken from the parable, but from our Lord's own explanation of the parable. In this verse, we are distinctly told that there is a person called *"the wicked one"* who *"snatches away"* the Word of God from hearts that do not understand and heed it.

If Satan were not a real person, and if our Lord had only been referring to evil forces or even human influences as snatching away the Word from hearts, His words in Matthew 13:19 would not make any sense. But Jesus Christ believed that there is a person called Satan. He referred to him here as *"the wicked one,"* and He referred to him elsewhere, as we will soon see, as "the Devil." If we grant that the Lord Jesus was an honest man, we can have no doubt that He believed there is a literal Devil. Therefore, if we believe in the Lord Jesus, we must also believe that there is a Devil. We can deny his existence only by questioning either the honesty or the intelligence of our Lord.

I could also easily show from the teachings of Peter (1 Pet. 5:8–9; Acts 5:3) and from the teachings of John (John 13:2) and from the teachings of Paul (Eph. 6:10–12) that there is a Devil. However, that is unnecessary for anyone who has any right to call himself a Christian, for if the Lord said it, that settles it, and the Lord Jesus did say, *"The devil...is."* If there is no Devil, then our Lord Jesus was either a fool or a fraud.

Clearly, the question of believing in the existence of a literal Devil involves the honor of our Lord Jesus. If His teaching is not to be trusted on this point, it is not to be trusted on any other point. To deny a literal Devil is to deny the trustworthiness of the Lord Jesus as a Teacher and as a Savior at every point. So we see that the question of the existence of the Devil is of fundamental and vital importance.

The Nature of the Devil

Having settled that there is a Devil, we now face the question of the nature of the Devil.

The Devil Is a Person

First of all, the Bible teaches us that the Devil is a person. This truth comes out in our second text, 1 John 3:8: *"The devil has sinned."* Only a person can sin. When I say that the Devil is a person, I do not mean that he necessarily has a body—and I certainly do not mean that he has the kind of body that he is pictured as having in various paintings. The definition of a person is "any being who knows and feels and wills." When I say that the Devil is a person, I mean that he is a being who has intelligence, feeling, and will—that he is not a mere "principle of evil."

The personhood of the Devil is taught over and over again in the Bible. I will give just a few illustrations in addition to our texts. Looking again at Matthew 13:19, we read,

> *When anyone hears the word of the kingdom, and does not understand it, then the wicked one comes and snatches away what was sown in his heart.*

The entity spoken of in this passage is a person. He is called by the name *"the wicked one"*—not merely "wickedness," but *"the wicked one"*—which of course represents a person.

The personhood of the Devil is shown again very clearly and very forcibly in Ephesians 6:10–12:

> *Finally, my brethren, be strong in the Lord and in the power of His might. Put on the whole armor of God, that you may be able to stand against the wiles of the devil. For we do not wrestle against flesh and blood, but against principalities, against powers, against the rulers of the darkness of this age, against spiritual hosts of wickedness in the heavenly places.*

Here Paul distinctly told us that the big reason that we need to be *"strong in the Lord"* and to *"put on the whole armor of God"* is that there is a being of great cunning, subtlety, and power, a person named *"the devil."* Furthermore, this being has under him a multitude of other persons, who have such rank and power that they are called by the titles *"principalities," "powers," "rulers," "spiritual hosts of wickedness."*

Beyond a question, our Lord Jesus, along with the apostles Peter, John, and Paul, believed in and taught the existence of a literal Devil. If there is not a literal Devil, we may as well give up the Bible, for in that case it is a book that is full of foolishness and fraud. If there is not a real Devil, we must give up our belief in the inspired authority of the apostles Peter, John, and Paul, and we must give up our faith in the Lord Jesus Christ. No intelligent student of the Bible can retain his faith in the inspiration and authority of that Book, or his faith in the Lord Jesus Christ, if he gives up his belief in the existence of a literal Devil. As intelligent men and women, we must make our choice between believing in the existence of a literal Devil and giving up our faith in Jesus Christ and Christianity. Any system of doctrine that denies the existence of a real Devil is radically unchristian, no matter what name it may claim for itself.

The Devil Is Powerful

The second thing that the Bible teaches about the nature of the Devil is that the Devil is a being of great power and authority. This fact comes out in two of the verses we have just read, Ephesians 6:10–11:

> *Finally, my brethren, be strong in the Lord and in the power of His might. Put on the whole armor of God, that you may be able to stand against the wiles of the devil.*

These words make it clear that the Devil is so mighty that God's people cannot resist his power and cunning schemes without being clothed with the armor of God and being strengthened with the strength of God.

This is not all. In the twelfth verse, we read,

> *For we do not wrestle against flesh and blood, but against principalities, against powers, against the rulers of the darkness of this age, against spiritual hosts of wickedness in the heavenly places.*

These are tremendous words. If they mean anything, they certainly mean that there are beings of great authority and rank who are under the leadership of the one supreme being of evil, the Devil.

The conflict that we have on hand as believers in Christ is terrific. Any international military conflict that could arise is nothing in comparison with the battle that we have on hand with the Devil and his hosts. We are fools if we underestimate the fight.

On the other hand, we must not overestimate it. While our conflict is with the Devil, and while our wrestling is against the *"principalities,"* the *"powers,"* the *"rulers,"* and the *"spiritual hosts of wickedness,"*

He who is for us is far mightier than they (1 John 4:4). The Devil is mighty, but our Savior is almighty. It is quite possible for a person to become morbid over this subject of the Devil, and to become utterly discouraged and even deranged. This extreme is entirely unnecessary and unwarranted. While our conflict is with the Devil and his mighty hosts, God has provided for us a strength and an armor whereby we may *"quench all the fiery darts of the wicked one"* (Eph. 6:16) and *"withstand in the evil day, and having done all, to stand"* (v. 13).

The Devil Has an Exalted Position

The third thing that the Bible teaches about the nature of the Devil is that the Devil is a being of grandeur and rank. We read in Jude 8–9,

> *Likewise also these dreamers defile the flesh, reject authority, and speak evil of dignitaries* [the literal translation of the Greek word rendered *"dignitaries"* is "glories"]. *Yet Michael the archangel, in contending with the devil, when he disputed about the body of Moses, dared not bring against him a reviling accusation, but said, "The Lord rebuke you!"*

From these words, it is evident that the position of the Devil was so exalted that even Michael the archangel did not dare to bring *"a reviling accusation"* against him. The context seems to imply that the position of the Devil was more exalted than that of Michael the archangel himself.

The Devil in God's Word is not at all the Devil that is commonly portrayed. He is not hideous in appearance, with hooves and horns and tail. He is not even the being pictured by Milton or Bunyan. He is a being of great original majesty and dignity, a being of great wisdom and power. When people talk lightly and contemptuously of the Devil, they display gross ignorance of what the Bible teaches about him. It is true that he is wicked in character and is therefore called *"the wicked one"* (1 John 5:19). It is true that he is a liar and a murderer (John 8:44). It is true that he is full of malignity. (See 2 Corinthians 4:4.) But he is a being of grandeur and rank, so that even Michael the archangel did not dare to bring an abusive accusation against him.

The Devil Is the Ruler of the Present World Order

Furthermore, the Bible teaches that the Devil is *"the prince of this world."* Our Lord Jesus Himself taught this fact. He said in John 12:31, *"Now is the judgment of this world: now shall the prince of this world be cast out"* (KJV). The Greek word translated *"world"* in this passage is *kosmos,* which refers to the present world order. Our Lord's teaching is that the Devil is the prince of this present world order.

Jesus taught the same thing in John 14:30, on the evening before His crucifixion: *"I will no longer talk much with you, for the ruler of this world is coming, and he has nothing in Me."* These words of Jesus Christ are found in what many people regard as the most precious chapter in the Bible, the fourteenth chapter of John. If we give up this teaching of our Lord regarding Satan, we must give up this most precious chapter and, indeed, the entire Bible. We find Jesus teaching the same thing again on that same night, the night before His crucifixion, in John 16:11: *"The ruler of this world is judged,"* the evident reference being to Satan.

How the Devil came to be *"the prince of this world"* it may be impossible for us to say, but if we are to accept the teaching of Jesus Christ, there is no question that he is so. To anyone who studies the ruling principles of economic life, political life, social life, and above all, international relations, it becomes perfectly evident that the Devil is the one who is the master of the present order of things. If we ever doubted before that there is a Devil, and just such a Devil as the Bible describes, we can scarcely doubt it now, when we consider the actions of the rulers of this earth. How could beings so intelligent in matters of science and philosophy and economics, ever be guilty of plunging the nations of the earth into war? There is only one reasonable answer: because there is a Devil who rules the present kosmos, or world order, and he controls the evil rulers of the world and will continue to control them until the true Prince comes, the Prince of Peace, our Lord Jesus Christ.

The Character of the Devil

As for the character of the Devil, the Bible teaches us that he is a being who is absolutely wicked. In Matthew 13:19, he is called *"the wicked one"*; that is, he is the person who is the embodiment of absolute wickedness. First John 5:19 also calls him *"the wicked one."* God, on the other hand, is called *"the Holy One"* throughout the Bible; that is, He is the Person who is the embodiment of perfect holiness. Simply put, the Devil is the opposite of God. The Devil is to evil what God is to good.

In 1 John 3:8, we read,

He who sins is of the devil, for the devil has sinned from the beginning. For this purpose the Son of God was manifested, that He might destroy the works of the devil.

This verse does not mean that the Devil has sinned from the very origin of all things and that he was created sinful, for we learn from Ezekiel 28:15 that the Devil was created upright. The expression *"from the beginning"* is characteristic of the epistle from which these words are taken and does not necessarily mean from the origin of things. (See, for example, 1 John 3:11.) This verse does mean, however, that Satan is the original sinner.

In a similar way, we are told in John 8:44 that the Devil *"was a murderer from the beginning,"* and that *"he is a liar and the father of it."* There is absolutely *"no truth in him"* (v. 44). This is the character of the Devil.

The Work of the Devil

We now come to the question of the work of the Devil, or how the Devil manifests himself and what he does.

The Devil Is the Tempter

First of all, we are taught that the Devil tempts people to sin. We have a most striking illustration of this in his temptation of our Lord. There are three accounts of this temptation in the Bible. We will look at Matthew's account:

> *Then Jesus was led up by the Spirit into the wilderness to be tempted by the devil. And when He had fasted forty days and forty nights, afterward He was hungry. Now when the tempter came to Him, he said, "If You are the Son of God, command that these stones become bread." But He answered and said, "It is written, 'Man shall not live by bread alone, but by every word that proceeds from the mouth of God.'" Then the devil took Him up into the holy city, set Him on the pinnacle of the temple, and said to Him, "If You are the Son of God, throw Yourself down. For it is written: 'He shall give His angels charge over you,' and, 'In their hands they shall bear you up, lest you dash your foot against a stone.'" Jesus said to him, "It is written again, 'You shall not tempt the LORD your God.'" Again, the devil took Him up on an exceedingly high mountain, and showed Him all the kingdoms of the world and their glory. And he said to Him, "All these things I will give You if You will fall down and worship me." Then Jesus said to him, "Away with you, Satan! For it is written, 'You shall worship the LORD your God, and Him only you shall serve.'" Then the devil left Him, and behold, angels came and ministered to Him.* (Matt. 4:1–11)

Of course, it would require a long study to go into the whole matter of our Lord's temptation, but this much is certainly plain: the Devil is represented as the Tempter. If there is no literal Devil, as so many would have us believe, or if he is not the Tempter, there would be absolutely no reason for bringing him into this account.

As the Devil tempted our Lord, so he tempts us today. Notice that he does not tempt us merely with gross animal lusts and vile sins, but with subtle spiritual temptations. Above all, he tempts us to doubt God's Word. It was with this form of temptation that he first assaulted Jesus. God had just said to our Lord at His baptism, *"You are My beloved Son; in You I am well pleased"* (Luke 3:22). Satan tried to cause Christ to doubt what God had said by beginning his temptation with these words: *"If You are the Son of God...."* Again, later on in his temptation of Christ, he repeated the doubt, saying to the Lord Jesus, *"If You are the Son of God...."*

In exactly the same way, Satan began his assault on Eve in the Garden of Eden. He introduced a doubt of God's Word and God's goodness. He began by saying, *"Has God indeed said...?"* (Gen. 3:1), and later on, when Eve stated exactly what God had said, the Devil flatly contradicted Him and said, *"You will not surely die* [literally, "dying, you will not die"]" (v. 4), when God had said, *"You shall surely die* ["dying, you will die"]" (Gen. 2:17).

Satan's favorite and most effective method of attack today is to get us to doubt God's Word, to lead us into doubt and error on fundamental points. The bars, the casinos, and the houses of prostitution are not the chief spheres of Satan's activities. His primary fields are the schools, colleges, and theological seminaries, where he is inducing men, women, and children to doubt the truth of God's Word. The Devil tempts them to reject the fundamental truths of God's Word and to accept his errors in their place. He knows very well that if he can get people to doubt God's Word, it is easy to lead them into the vilest of sins. False doctrine has been a more prolific source of the vilest sins than even the barrooms.

The Devil Uses Churches and Ministers

Not only does Satan tempt people to sin by introducing doubts of God's Word, but he also has his churches and ministers to do his work. We find this fact in Revelation 3:9:

> *Indeed I will make those of the synagogue of Satan, who say they are Jews and are not, but lie; indeed I will make them come and worship before your feet, and to know that I have loved you.*

What I want you to notice here are the words *"the synagogue of Satan."* In this case, Satan's tool was a Jewish synagogue, but nowadays, it is often a so-called Christian church.

In 2 Corinthians 11:14–15, we have an even more remarkable passage:

> *For Satan himself transforms himself into an angel of light. Therefore it is no great thing if his ministers also transform themselves into ministers of righteousness, whose end will be according to their works.*

Here we are told that Satan has his ministers. They do not advertise themselves as such. Oftentimes they are not even aware that they are Satan's ministers; instead, they promote themselves as *"ministers of righteousness."* Satan's ministers advocate a system of salvation without atoning blood. They are frequently men and women with very attractive personalities and great intelligence, but they are doing the Devil's work.

Satan is never so dangerous as when he *"transforms himself into an angel of light."* Furthermore, no ministers of his are so dangerous as the men and women with pleasing personalities and brilliant minds who are undermining the faith of God's children. Many of Satan's ministers are teaching various forms of seductive and alluring error through Christian Science, New Thought, Theosophy, occultism (Spiritualism), and other cults.

The Devil Blinds People to the Truth about Jesus

Satan is also the author of sickness (Acts 10:38; Luke 13:16) and the author of death (Heb. 2:14). But I must also tell about another task of the Devil. It is found in 2 Corinthians 4:3–4:

> *But even if our gospel is veiled, it is veiled to those who are perishing, whose minds the god of this age has blinded, who do not believe, lest the light of the gospel of the glory of Christ, who is the image of God, should shine on them.*

We read here that it is the work of Satan to blind the minds of unbelievers *"lest the light of the gospel of the glory of Christ, who is the image of God, should shine on them."*

It is evident, then, that the Devil is the originator of false views, especially false views of the person of Christ. He is the author of Unitarianism, along with all the various forms of the denial of Christ's deity. He so blinds the minds of men who submit to his working that the divine *"glory of Christ,"* who is the very *"image of God,"* is hidden from them. This fact explains why Unitarianism persists in all its various forms, even after its foolishness has been so often exposed.

Satan's work along these lines will culminate at the appearing of the Antichrist:

> *The coming of the lawless one* [the Antichrist] *is according to the working of Satan, with all power, signs, and lying wonders, and with all unrighteous deception among those who perish, because they did not receive the love of the truth, that they might be saved.*
> *(2 Thess. 2:9–10)*

The Destiny of the Devil

We now come to the fifth topic of our subject— the Devil's destiny.

First, we will look at Revelation 20:1–3:

> *Then I saw an angel coming down from heaven, having the key to the bottomless pit and a great chain in his hand. He laid hold of the dragon, that serpent of old, who is the Devil and Satan, and bound him for a thousand*

*years; and he cast him into the bottomless pit,
and shut him up, and set a seal on him, so
that he should deceive the nations no more till
the thousand years were finished. But after
these things he must be released for a little
while.*

At the second coming of our Lord Jesus Christ, Satan will be bound with a great chain and cast into
"the bottomless pit" for a thousand years. *"The bottomless pit"* does not mean hell, but we will soon see
that Satan will later be cast into hell.

Second, let us consider Revelation 20:7–8:

*Now when the thousand years have expired,
Satan will be released from his prison and
will go out to deceive the nations which are in
the four corners of the earth, Gog and Magog,
to gather them together to battle, whose number is as the sand of the sea.*

In these verses, we are taught that at the end of the
Millennium, the thousand-year reign of Christ on
earth, Satan will be loosed for a short season from
his bondage and from the bottomless pit into which
he has been cast. He will come forth to deceive the
nations, but the time of his power will be brief.

Third, in Revelation 20:10, we find the ultimate
destiny of the Devil:

*The devil, who deceived them, was cast into
the lake of fire and brimstone where the beast
and the false prophet are. And they will be
tormented day and night forever and ever.*

139

Here is one of the points at which the theories of the Universalists* generally break down. The argument of the Universalists, by which they attempt to prove that everyone must ultimately be saved, carried to its logical conclusion, would also prove the salvation of Satan. Many of them do plainly say that the Devil will ultimately be brought to repentance and be saved. Indeed, that is what I believed and taught in my early ministry. But the passage that we have just read shows the impossibility of this being true, for the Devil will go to the lake of fire.

Our Lord Himself said that when He comes back to judge this world, He will say to the unbelievers, *"Depart from Me, you cursed, into the everlasting fire prepared for the devil and his angels"* (Matt. 25:41). Hell was not prepared for people but for the Devil and his angels. The only reason that any person will go there will be that he has chosen to cast in his lot with the Devil rather than with God. Therefore, he will go where the Devil goes. Everyone who rejects Jesus Christ is throwing in his lot with Satan.

How to Be Victorious over the Devil

Now let me briefly show you from the Word of God how to get the victory over the Devil in practical, everyday life. There are four things to keep in mind.

First, James 4:7 says, *"Therefore submit to God. Resist the devil and he will flee from you."* This

---

* The main tenet of Universalism is that eventually everyone will be saved. Universalism began in the eighteenth century and later united with Unitarianism.

teaches us that we are first of all to surrender to God and then resist the Devil. In spite of all Satan's cunning and power, if we do resist him, he will flee from us. Although the Devil is strong, it is our privilege in God's strength to withstand him and overcome him.

Second, we read in 1 John 2:14,

> *I have written to you, fathers, because you have known Him who is from the beginning. I have written to you, young men, because you are strong, and the word of God abides in you, and you have overcome the wicked one.*

This passage teaches us that when we feed upon the Word of God and store the Word of God in our hearts, thus having it abide in us, we will be able to overcome the Devil. If we neglect the study of the Bible for a single day, we leave an open door for the Devil. I have been a Christian for forty-three years, but I would not dare to neglect the study of God's Word for one single day. Why not? Because there is a Devil; and if I neglect the study of the Word of God for a single day, I leave a window open through which he can enter, and I leave myself too weak to cope with him and to conquer him. But if we will feed upon the Word of God daily and trust in God, we can resist the Devil at every point. Though the Devil is cunning and strong, God is stronger, and God imparts His strength to us through His written Word.

Third, we are told in Ephesians 6:11, *"Put on the whole armor of God, that you may be able to stand against the wiles of the devil."* Here we are taught that in order to stand against Satan's schemes, we must *"put on the whole armor of God."* We find what that armor is in the verses that immediately follow.

This armor, this panoply of God, is at our disposal. The fact that there is a Devil, that he is a being of such grandeur, dignity, cunning, and power, that he is incessantly plotting to ruin us and to undermine our faith, is no reason for fear or discouragement. By taking *"the shield of faith,"* we *"will be able to quench all the fiery darts of the wicked one"* (Eph. 6:16). By taking *"the helmet of salvation, and the sword of the Spirit, which is the word of God"* (v. 17), and by *"praying always with all prayer and supplication in the Spirit"* (v. 18), it is our privilege to have victory over the Devil every day of our lives—every hour of the day, and every minute of the hour.

The fourth and final step in the plan to get victory over Satan is found in Ephesians 6:10: *"Finally, my brethren, be strong in the Lord and in the power of His might."* The way to get victory over Satan is to give up all confidence in our own strength, to believe in the almighty strength of Jesus Christ, and to claim that strength for ourselves. It is in the strength of Jesus Christ's might that we will get the victory over the Evil One. In the strength of His might, as I have already said, it is our privilege to have victory over the Devil every minute of our lives. Hallelujah!

Seven

Is There a Literal Hell?

Is There a Literal Hell?

In danger of hell fire.
—Matthew 5:22

I wish that the things that I am going to write in this chapter were not true. God wishes so, too. *"The Lord...is longsuffering toward us, not willing that any should perish but that all should come to repentance"* (2 Pet. 3:9). But God has made us in His own image—with a moral nature, with a capacity for decision, with a power of choice. People can, if they want, choose darkness instead of light. They can choose to trample God's saving love underfoot. They can choose to reject the One who was *"wounded for* [their] *transgressions"* and *"bruised for* [their] *iniquities"* (Isa. 53:5).

Some people will make this choice. I am sorry that they will—so sorry that I would be willing to die to save them. The Lord Jesus did die to save them, but they spurn Him.

The things that I am about to tell you about hell are true, and I am going to explain them in order that you may be certain of them. I am writing about hell in order to keep as many of you as possible from going there.

Is there a literal hell? Almost all intelligent people who believe that there is a future life at all believe that there is future punishment. They agree that men and women who sin in the present life and who die impenitent will be punished in the future life, at least to some extent. They admit that whoever sins must suffer, and that the suffering that sin causes will not be limited to our earthly existence.

But while almost all intelligent people who believe in the afterlife believe that there is some kind of future punishment, many of them do not believe in a literal hell, that is, a place of awful and unutterable torment.

Is there a hell? Is there a place to which impenitent men and women will go sometime after death and suffer agonies far beyond those that anyone suffers here on earth? Some say, "Yes, there is a hell." Yet many preachers, even supposedly sound preachers, say, "No, the only hell is the inward hell in a man's heart." So how are we to settle this question? How are we to determine who is right?

We cannot settle it as some are trying to do, by consensus. Majorities are not always right, especially in matters of science, philosophy, and theology. What the majority of scientists firmly believed a century ago, the majority of scientists laugh at today. What the majority of philosophers once believed, the majority of philosophers today regard as ridiculous. Therefore, we cannot settle this question by asking what the majority believe.

Nor can we settle it by our own human reasoning. How can finite and foolish man judge what an infinitely holy and infinitely wise God would do? Man never appears more foolish than when he tries to use his own thoughts to reach conclusions in this matter. All these arguments about hell that result from reasoning as to what God must or must not do are stupid. A child of seven cannot reason infallibly as to what a wise and good man of fifty would do. Much less can puny creatures of the dust (such as you and I, such as the most educated philosophers and theologians) reason infallibly as to what a wise and good God must do.

However, with the wars and atrocities happening around us in the world, it is far easier today to believe in a literal and everlasting hell from the standpoint of pure reasoning than it was in past centuries. Nevertheless, even today we cannot settle this matter by reasoning as to what such a being as God must do.

There is only one way to settle this question properly, and that is by going to the Bible, finding out what it says, and taking our stand firmly and unhesitatingly upon that. We know that the Bible is, beyond a doubt, God's Word,* so whatever the Bible says on this subject, or any other subject, is true and certain.

It is especially true that we must go to the Bible to find what it says in the matter of future punishment and future blessedness. All we know about the future is what the Bible tells us. All reasoning about the future outside of what the Bible tells us is pure

---

* For an in-depth discussion on the inspiration of the Bible, see Torrey's book *God, the Bible, and You* (New Kensington, PA: Whitaker House, 1999).

guessing; it is a waste of time. We know nothing about heaven except what God's Word says, and we know nothing about hell except what God's Word says. On a subject like this, one ounce of God's revelation is worth a thousand tons of man's speculation. The whole question is, What does the Bible say about hell?

Not only are we dependent entirely on the Bible, but the Bible clearly reveals all that we need to know. The Bible tells us a great deal about heaven and still more about hell. It is an interesting fact that the Lord Jesus Himself, whose words many are ready to accept even though they may reject the authority of the rest of the Bible, is the One who told us the most about hell—and the One who told us the most clearly about hell. Indeed, most of what I am going to show you is what the Lord Jesus Himself said on this subject.

What Is the Difference between Hell and Hades?

First of all, in order to clear the way for our study of what Jesus said on this subject, let me call your attention to the fact that hell and hades are not the same. The word that is translated *hell* in many verses in the King James Version is translated *hades* in these verses in other Bible versions. These other versions are right on this point, as every Greek scholar knows. Hades is not hell. Hades is the Greek equivalent of the Old Testament Hebrew word *sheol*. This Hebrew word *sheol* is frequently translated in the King James Version of the Old Testament as *grave*. It should never be translated in this way, since it never means grave. I have taken the pains to look up every passage where this Hebrew word is used, and in not a single instance does it mean grave. There is an entirely different Hebrew word that can properly be translated in that way. *Sheol,* or the New Testament word *hades,* means "the place of departed spirits."

Before the birth, life, death, resurrection, and ascension of our Lord, sheol (or hades) was the place where all the spirits of the dead—both good and bad—went. Before the ascension of Christ, hades contained both paradise, the abode of the blessed dead, and the *"place of torment"* (Luke 16:28), the abode of the wicked dead. At His ascension, Christ emptied the paradise of hades and took its inhabitants up to heaven with Him, as we read in Ephesians 4:8: *"When He ascended on high, He led captivity captive, and gave gifts to men."*

Before Christ ascended, paradise was in sheol; now it is in heaven. Christ said to the repentant thief on the cross, *"Assuredly, I say to you, today you will be with Me in Paradise"* (Luke 23:43), and Jesus Himself taught us that He went down into *"the heart of the earth"* (Matt. 12:40). The dying thief went down with Him into this subterranean paradise. I think Jesus Himself also went into that part of hades where the lost spirits were (see 1 Peter 3:18–20), but that is another story. All that is important now is that the repentant, dying thief went *down* into paradise with Christ but was taken to heaven when Christ ascended there. Note that, after the ascension of the Lord, when Paul wrote that he had gone to paradise, he said that he had been *"caught **up** to the third heaven...into Paradise"* (2 Cor. 12:2, 4, emphasis added).

No blessed dead are now left in hades, and ultimately, *"Death"* and *"Hades"* (that is, all the dead who have not been caught up into the celestial paradise—all of whom are still in hades) will be *"cast into the lake of fire"* (Rev. 20:14). This *"lake of fire"* into which death and hades are to be cast is the true and ultimate hell.

Is There a Literal Hell?

Having cleared the way by removing the misunderstanding so common in the minds of people today that hades and hell are the same, let me say next that there is a literal hell. The Bible says so. Jesus said in Matthew 5:22,

> *I say to you that whoever is angry with his brother without a cause shall be in danger of the judgment. And whoever says to his brother, "Raca!"* [a strong term of derision] *shall be in danger of the council. But whoever says, "You fool!" shall be in danger of hell fire.*

In the twenty-ninth verse of the same chapter, the Lord Jesus said,

> *If your right eye causes you to sin, pluck it out and cast it from you; for it is more profitable for you that one of your members perish, than for your whole body to be cast into hell.*

And in the thirtieth verse, He said,

> *And if your right hand causes you to sin, cut it off and cast it from you; for it is more profitable*

*for you that one of your members perish, than
for your whole body to be cast into hell.*

Mark 9:45, 47–48 repeats this teaching of Jesus:

*And if your foot causes you to sin, cut it off. It
is better for you to enter life lame, rather than
having two feet, to be cast into hell....And if
your eye causes you to sin, pluck it out. It is
better for you to enter the kingdom of God with
one eye, rather than having two eyes, to be cast
into hell fire; where "Their worm does not die,
and the fire is not quenched."*

Someone may say that these words of our Lord
are figurative, but there is not the slightest hint that
this is so. The context of each of these passages is
against their being taken figuratively. It is indeed
wrong to interpret figurative language as if it were
literal, but it is just as wrong to interpret literal language as if it were figurative.

Of course, the word *gehenna,* which is translated *"hell"* in these passages, is derived from the
name of a valley of Jerusalem, the valley of Hinnom,
where in ancient times human sacrifices were offered. But the *use* of the word is literal throughout
the New Testament, even though its *derivation* is
figurative. Many words that are figurative in their
derivation are literal in their use, and the meaning
of words is never determined by derivation but by
usage. For example, our word *eclipse* is a figure of
speech. Figuratively, it means a "leaving" or
"failing" or "fainting" of the moon or sun, whichever
it may be that is eclipsed. But though the word is

figurative in its derivation, the ordinary usage of it is literal.

In the New Testament, the universal use of *gehenna,* or *"hell,"* is literal. *Gehenna* is found twelve times in the New Testament, and eleven of these twelve times it is used by our Lord Jesus Himself. He uniformly used it, as in the passages that I have just read, concerning a literal hell.

If we go to Christ's words to discover their natural meaning, there can be no doubt that He meant to convey the impression that there is a literal hell. If there is no literal hell, then either Jesus thought there was one when there is not, in which case He was a fool; or He thought that hell does not exist but tried to make men think that it does, in which case He was a fraud. There is no other alternative. We must believe that there is a literal hell or else believe that Jesus of Nazareth, our Lord and Savior, was a fool or a fraud.

I know that Jesus was not senseless or deceptive. I know that He was the *"only begotten Son"* of God (John 3:16), that *"in Him dwells all the fullness of the Godhead bodily"* (Col. 2:9), that He and the Father are one (John 10:30), that *"all should honor the Son just as they honor the Father"* (John 5:23). I know that He spoke the very words of God; therefore, I know that there is a literal hell.

Furthermore, it is noteworthy that most of these words about hell that I have quoted from Scripture are taken from the Sermon on the Mount, the one part of Scripture that most people who are familiar with the Bible claim to believe. There are many who say that they do not know about the reliability of the Bible as a whole but who do accept the

Sermon on the Mount. Since most of these passages
are from the Sermon on the Mount, we must either
accept these parts of the Sermon or throw the whole
thing overboard as the utterance of a fool or a fraud.
There is no other choice possible for anyone who is
willing to think things through.

Is the Fire of Hell Literal Fire?

The next question that confronts us is, Is the
hellfire mentioned in some of the passages we have
read literal fire? This is not as vital a question as, Is
there is a literal hell? but it is nevertheless important. I believe the question is plainly answered in
the Bible by Jesus Christ Himself. Referring again to
Matthew 5:22, we read,

> *I say to you that whoever is angry with his
> brother without a cause shall be in danger of
> the judgment. And whoever says to his brother,
> "Raca!"* [a strong term of derision] *shall be in
> danger of the council. But whoever says, "You
> fool!" shall be in danger of hell fire.*

These are Christ's own words. He speaks not only of
hell, but *"hell fire,"* and this verse, too, is from the
Sermon on the Mount.

In Matthew 18:9, the Lord Jesus said again,

> *And if your eye causes you to sin, pluck it out
> and cast it from you. It is better for you to enter
> into life with one eye, rather than having two
> eyes, to be cast into hell fire.*

And in Mark 9:43, 45, 47–48, most of which I quoted earlier in this chapter, we read,

> *If your hand causes you to sin, cut it off. It is better for you to enter into life maimed, rather than having two hands, to go to hell, into the fire that shall never be quenched....And if your foot causes you to sin, cut it off. It is better for you to enter life lame, rather than having two feet, to be cast into hell....And if your eye causes you to sin, pluck it out. It is better for you to enter the kingdom of God with one eye, rather than having two eyes, to be cast into hell fire; where "Their worm does not die, and the fire is not quenched."*

Here again, some may say the fire is figurative. But in Matthew 13:30, we read these words:

> *Let both grow together until the harvest, and at the time of harvest I will say to the reapers, "First gather together the tares and bind them in bundles to burn them, but gather the wheat into my barn."*

Now, this verse is part of a parable, which has symbolic language. There would be warrant, if this verse were all that we had, for saying that the fire is figurative, just as the other things in the verse are figurative. But in the forty-first and forty-second verses of the same chapter, we read,

> *The Son of Man will send out His angels, and they will gather out of His kingdom all things*

> *that offend, and those who practice lawless-*
> *ness, and will cast them into the furnace of*
> *fire. There will be wailing and gnashing of*
> *teeth.*

Here we have the *interpretation* of the parable.

Now, in parables, as I have already said, we have symbols; but in the interpretation of parables, we have the literal facts that the symbols represent. We see clearly that here in the interpretation, as well as in the parable, we have fire. Everything else in the parable is explained—every item in the parable except the fire. The fire in the parable remains fire in the interpretation.

We find the same teaching in another parable, in Matthew 13:47–50—the parable of the net:

> *Again, the kingdom of heaven is like a dragnet*
> *that was cast into the sea and gathered some*
> *of every kind, which, when it was full, they*
> *drew to shore; and they sat down and gathered*
> *the good into vessels, but threw the bad away.*
> *So it will be at the end of the age. The angels*
> *will come forth, separate the wicked from*
> *among the just, and cast them into the furnace*
> *of fire. There will be wailing and gnashing of*
> *teeth.*

Here also, in the interpretation of the parable, we have fire.

Furthermore, we read in Revelation 20:15 that at the judgment of the Great White Throne, *"anyone not found written in the Book of Life was cast into the lake of fire."* There is nothing in the whole context that suggests that the lake of fire is a symbol. And in Revelation 21:8, we read,

> *But the cowardly, unbelieving, abominable, murderers, sexually immoral, sorcerers, idolaters, and all liars shall have their part in the lake which burns with fire and brimstone, which is the second death.*

In light of these facts, we cannot deny the literal fire of hell without doing violence to every reasonable law of interpretation.

Will People in Hell Have Bodies?

The wicked in the eternal world will not be mere disembodied spirits. This fact is plain from both the Old Testament and the New.

We read in Daniel 12:2, *"And many of **those who sleep in the dust of the earth** shall awake, some to everlasting life, some to shame and everlasting contempt"* (emphasis added). The soul of the wicked departs into hades; it is the *body* that crumbles into dust. So this verse is referring to the physical bodies that are going to be raised.

In the New Testament, in John 5:28–29, our Lord is recorded as saying,

> *Do not marvel at this; for the hour is coming in which all who are in the graves will hear His voice and come forth; those who have done good, to the resurrection of life, and those who have done evil, to the resurrection of condemnation.*

Now, it is not souls that are in the graves—it is bodies. This passage teaches the resurrection of bodies, both of the good and of the wicked.

In 1 Corinthians 15:22, we read, *"For as in Adam all die, even so in Christ all shall be made alive."* What Paul was talking about in this entire chapter is the resurrection of the *body,* not merely the immortality of the soul. Here we are distinctly told that every child of Adam will receive the resurrection of his body in Christ.

Furthermore, in Matthew 5:30, Jesus said,

> *And if your right hand causes you to sin, cut it off and cast it from you; for it is more profitable for you that one of your members perish, than for your whole body to be cast into hell.*

Here, in the plainest possible terms, the body is spoken of as going to hell.

In a similar way, in Matthew 10:28, the Lord Jesus said, *"Do not fear those who kill the body but cannot kill the soul. But rather fear Him who is able to destroy both soul and body in hell."* From these clear and definite words of our Lord, it is as plain as day that in the future life we are to have bodies, and that the bodies of the lost are to have a place in hell.

The bodily torments of hellfire are not the most appalling feature of hell. The mental agony—the agony of remorse, the agony of shame, and the agony of despair—is worse, immeasurably worse. Nevertheless, physical suffering—a physical suffering with which no pain on earth is anything in comparison—is a feature of hell.

Is the Lake of Fire a Place of Continued, Conscious Torment?

One other question remains to be answered: Is the lake of fire a place of conscious torment, a place of nonconscious existence, or a place of annihilation—that is, a place of nonexistence? There are those who believe in a literal hell but do not believe that those who are consigned to it will consciously suffer for any great length of time. They believe either that those who are sent to hell will be annihilated or that they will exist there in a nonconscious state.

Of course, this would still be an everlasting hell, and everlasting punishment, but is it the hell that is taught in the Bible? Is the lake of fire a place of continued, conscious torment? In answer to this question, let me call your attention to the fact that the punishment of the wicked is spoken of in the Bible most frequently as "death" and "destruction." But what do these words mean in biblical usage?

The Biblical Meaning of "Death"

First, let us look at the word *death.* I have been told by people time and time again that death means nonexistence, or at least nonconscious existence, and that therefore this is what it must mean in the passages where it is spoken of as the future punishment of the impenitent. But does death *as used in the Bible* mean either nonconscious existence or annihilation?

First of all, look at 1 Timothy 5:6: *"She who lives in pleasure is dead while she lives."* Death here certainly does not mean either nonexistence or non-conscious existence. The woman who lives in pleasure still exists, and she certainly exists consciously, but she is *"dead."* In a similar way, we are told in Ephesians 2:1 that until people are made alive by the power of God, they are *"dead in trespasses and sins."*

Death means wrong existence rather than non-existence. It is just the opposite of life, and life in New Testament usage does not mean mere existence—it means a right, Godlike, holy existence, the elevation and ennoblement and glorification of existence. Death means just the opposite. It means a wrong and debased existence—the ruin, the shame, the ignominy, and the despair of existence. It is perfectly clear, then, that when the Bible speaks of death, it does not mean either annihilation or non-conscious existence.

But even more decisive than these examples is the fact that God Himself has defined death very exactly and very fully in Revelation 21:8:

> *But the cowardly, unbelieving, abominable, murderers, sexually immoral, sorcerers, idola-ters, and all liars shall have their part in the lake which burns with fire and brimstone, which is the second death.*

Here we are told in so many words that the *"death"* that is the final outcome of persistent sin and unbe-lief is a portion in the place of torment, the lake of fire. That this lake of fire is a place of conscious suffering is made clear in the preceding chapter, in Revelation 20:10, where we are told,

The devil, who deceived them, was cast into the lake of fire and brimstone where the beast and the false prophet are. And they will be tormented day and night forever and ever.

The Beast and False Prophet will have already been in the lake of fire for a thousand years when the Devil is thrown there (see Revelation 19:20–20:3, 7–10), and they will have been tormented all that time. Then they will continue to be tormented consciously without rest, and Satan will be punished in the same way.

The Biblical Meaning of "Destruction"

Now let us look at what the word *destruction* means in the Bible. We are told by a certain school of religious thought that the biblical meaning of destruction is simply destruction. Yes, but what does destruction mean? They say it means annihilation, or ceasing to exist, but the Greek word so translated never means that in the Bible or even outside of the Bible. When we look at the root meaning, we see that the noun that is commonly translated *destruction* and *perdition* is derived from a verb that means "to perish." Therefore, we need to find out what the word *perish* means in the Bible. For this task, let us turn to the best Greek-English dictionary of the New Testament that exists—*Thayer's Greek-English Lexicon of the New Testament* (a translation of Grimm's great work). Here we are told that when a thing is said to "perish," it does not cease to exist, but it is "so ruined that it no longer subserves the use for which it was designed."

Furthermore, here again, God has been careful to define His terms. He Himself has given us in the Bible a definition of the term *destruction*. We read in Revelation 17:8, *"The beast that you saw was, and is not, and will ascend out of the bottomless pit and go to perdition."* Here we are told that the Beast will go *"to perdition."* The word here translated *"perdition"* is precisely the same word that is elsewhere translated *destruction,* and it should be so translated here. Or, in the other instances, it should be translated *"perdition."* Now, if we can find what the Beast will go into, we will know exactly what destruction means, for we are told that he will go "into destruction."

As we have already seen, Revelation 19:20 tells us exactly where the Beast will go:

> *Then the beast was captured, and with him the false prophet who worked signs in his presence, by which he deceived those who received the mark of the beast and those who worshiped his image. These two were cast alive into the lake of fire burning with brimstone.*

So we see that the destruction into which the Beast will go is a place in the lake that burns with fire and brimstone. As we saw earlier, the Beast and the False Prophet will be consciously tormented for a thousand years before they are joined by the Devil, and then they will continue to exist in conscious torment forever and ever. So then, the word *destruction* is clearly defined in the New Testament in the same way in which *death* is defined, as the condition of beings in a place of conscious torment.

In Revelation 14:10–11, we read regarding the person who worships the Beast and his image, and who receives his mark on his forehead or on his hand:

> *He himself shall also drink of the wine of the wrath of God, which is poured out full strength into the cup of His indignation. He shall be tormented with fire and brimstone in the presence of the holy angels and in the presence of the Lamb. And the smoke of their torment ascends forever and ever; and they have no rest day or night, who worship the beast and his image, and whoever receives the mark of his name.*

The Bible makes it as clear as language can make it that the lake of fire, to which *"anyone not found written in the Book of Life"* (Rev. 20:15) will be consigned, is a place of continued, conscious torment. There is no escaping the clear teaching of the Word of God, unless we throw our Bibles away and discredit the teaching of the apostles and the teaching of Jesus Christ Himself.

General Sherman said, "War is hell." Of course, in the way that Sherman meant this statement, it is true. In fact, it is far more true of war today than it was in the worst and most inexcusable phases of our Civil War. But even war today is not literally hell, for hell is incomparably more awful than the worst war.

This dreadful hell that we have been studying is the destiny of some of you reading this, unless you repent and accept the Lord Jesus Christ. Other appalling facts about hell we will examine in the next chapter, in which we will consider the question, Is the punishment of the wicked everlasting? But we have already seen enough to make any true Christian determine to work with all his might to save others from this awful hell. And we have seen enough to make every honest and sensible person reading this determine to escape this terrible hell at any cost.

Eight

Is Future
Punishment
Everlasting?

Is Future Punishment Everlasting?

And these will go away into everlasting punishment,
but the righteous into eternal life.
—Matthew 25:46

J esus Christ plainly taught that there is a literal hell and that this hell is a place of conscious suffering, suffering far beyond that experienced by anyone here in this present life. But we are faced with another issue of great importance: Is this future conscious suffering of the impenitent going to be endless?

Many who believe in a severe future punishment, and who indeed believe in a literal hell, nevertheless deny, or at least doubt, that this future hell will be endless. They usually acknowledge and teach that the suffering may go on for a long time, and perhaps for thousands of years, but they believe that it will end at last and that all people will ultimately come to repentance, accept Jesus Christ, and be saved.

What is the precise truth about this matter? Like the question, Is there a literal hell? we cannot decide this question by asking what the majority of supposedly reliable theologians believe, for majorities are often wrong, and minorities are often right. Nor can we use our reasoning to determine what such a being as God must do. As we have seen, it is impossible for finite and foolish humans such as we are, and such as the wisest philosophers and theologians are, to judge what an infinitely wise and infinitely holy God must do. All such reasonings are utterly futile and an absolute waste of time.

What the Bible Teaches about the Endlessness of Future Punishment

What I said about the Bible in the previous chapter, I will say again, for it bears repeating. All that we know about the future is what God has been pleased to tell us in His Word. The Bible is, beyond a question, the Word of God; therefore, what it has to say is true and absolutely sure. In this matter, as well as in all others, one ounce of God's revelation is worth more than a thousand tons of man's speculation. The whole question is, What does the Bible teach regarding future punishment?

What Does "Everlasting" Mean?

Let us turn, first of all, to the words of our Lord Jesus Himself in Matthew 25:46: *"And these* [the wicked] *will go away into everlasting punishment, but the righteous into eternal life."* The first question that confronts us in studying this passage is what the word *aionios,* which is here translated *"everlasting,"* means. Thayer carefully studied Greek words, their derivation, and their usage, and in *Thayer's Greek-English Lexicon of the New Testament,* he gave these three definitions of the word, and these three only: (1) "Without beginning or end, that which always has been and always will be"; (2) "Without beginning"; and (3) "Without end; never to cease; everlasting."

Some say that the word *aionios,* according to its derivation, means "age-lasting," and therefore may refer to a limited period of time. Even admitting this to be true, we should again bear in mind that the meaning of words is not determined by their derivation but by their usage. The most important question is not what the derivation of this word may be, but how the word is used in the New Testament.

Aionios is used seventy-two times in the New Testament. Forty-four of these seventy-two times it is used in the phrase "eternal life" or in the phrase "everlasting life." No one questions that everlasting life is endless. In connection with the word *life,* the word *age-lasting* (if that is the proper derivation of *aionios*) means "lasting through all ages; never ending."

Below I will list fourteen more instances of the Greek word *aionios* in the Bible:

1. Once *"eternal"* is used of the *"salvation"* Christ brings (Heb. 5:9), which is indisputably never ending.

2. Once the term *"everlasting home"* is used (Luke 16:9), referring to the home that the blessed are to have in the world to come; and, of course, this also is never ending.

3.   Once *"eternal"* is used to describe the *"weight of glory"* that awaits the believer who endures affliction for Christ in the present life (2 Cor. 4:17). In this case, again, by universal consent, *"eternal"* means endless.

4.   Once *"eternal"* is used to describe the *"house not made with hands"* that believers in Christ are to receive at the coming of the Lord Jesus (2 Cor. 5:1). Of course, this *"house not made with hands"* is everlasting. In fact, the very point that is being explained in 2 Corinthians 5:1–8 is the contrast between our present bodies, which are only for a brief time, and our resurrection bodies, which are to exist throughout all eternity.

5.   Once *"eternal"* is used to illustrate the future unseen things that will never end, contrasted with the present seen things that are for a season (2 Cor. 4:18). That these unseen things are unending is the very point that is being brought out in this verse.

6.   Once *"everlasting"* is used of the *"consolation"* given to us by *"our Lord Jesus Christ Himself, and our God and Father"* (2 Thess. 2:16), and this is certainly endless.

7.   Once *"eternal"* is used of the *"redemption"* that Jesus Christ secured for us by His blood (Heb. 9:12). This redemption is never ending. In fact, the chief point of contrast in the context in this case is between the *temporary* redemption secured

by the constantly repeated sacrifices of the Mosaic ritual and the *never ending* redemption secured by the perfect sacrifice of Christ *"once for all"* (v. 12).

8. Once *"eternal"* is used of the *"inheritance"* that those who are in Christ receive (Heb. 9:15). Here again, beyond a question, it is unending.

9. Once *"everlasting"* is used of the *"covenant"* through Christ's blood (Heb. 13:20), which is contrasted with the *temporary* covenant, based on the blood of bulls and goats, given through Moses. Here again, *"everlasting"* necessarily and emphatically means never ending. This is the very point being discussed in the book of Hebrews.

10. Once *"everlasting"* is used of the *"kingdom of our Lord and Savior Jesus Christ"* (2 Pet. 1:11), and we are told in Luke 1:33, *"Of His kingdom there will be no end."*

11. Once *"everlasting"* is used of *"gospel"* (or Good News), and this, of course, never ends (Rev. 14:6).

12. Once *"everlasting"* is used of *"God"* (Rom. 16:26), and He certainly endures, not merely through long ages, but without end.

13. Once *"eternal"* is used of the *"Spirit"* (Heb. 9:14), and He also certainly endures throughout an absolutely endless eternity.

14. Twice *"eternal"* is used of the *"glory"* that those
    in Christ obtain (2 Tim. 2:10; 1 Pet. 5:10). This,
    of course, by universal consent, is endless.

We have covered fifty-nine of the seventy-two
times the Greek word *aionios* is used in the Bible. In
these fifty-nine instances, the idea of endlessness is
absolutely necessary to the meaning, and in not a
single one of the thirteen remaining places where
the word is used is it used of anything that is known
to end. If usage can determine the meaning of any
word, certainly the New Testament use of this word
determines it to mean "never ending," or, as Thayer
defined it, "without end; never to cease; everlasting."

Nor is this all. God Himself defines *aionios* as
never ending by specifically using it in contrast with
that which does end. One example that we have already noticed is 2 Corinthians 4:18, where we read,

> *While we do not look at the things which are
> seen, but at the things which are not seen. For
> the things which are seen are temporary*
> [literally, "for a season"], *but the things which
> are not seen are eternal.*

Here the whole point is that the unseen things—as
distinct from the seen, which are for a season—are
for a never ending duration.

But suppose we conceded that the word *aionios*
could be used to describe that which, though it may
last throughout an age, or ages, has an end. Even if
that were true (which it is not), the meaning of the
word in any given instance would have to be determined by the context in which it is found.

Now, what is the context in the passage that we are studying? Let us read it again: *"And these will go away into everlasting* [aionios] *punishment, but the righteous into eternal* [aionios] *life"* (Matt. 25:46). The same Greek adjective, *aionios,* is used in connection with *"punishment"* and with *"life."* Certainly, this qualifying adjective must have the same meaning in the one half of the sentence that it has in the other half of the sentence.

We must at least admit that Jesus Christ was an honest man, and He certainly was too honest to juggle with words. He would not use a word to mean one thing in one half of a sentence and something entirely different in the other half. He obviously sought to convey the impression that the punishment of the unsaved is of the same duration as the life of the saved.

No one questions that the life of the saved is endless. If it were not endless, all our hopes would be destroyed. Therefore, if we are to deal honestly with our Lord's words, we must believe that He taught that the punishment of the unsaved is going to be endless. We have exactly the same reason in God's Word for believing in unending punishment that we have for believing in unending life. If you give up the one, you must give up the other, or else deal dishonestly with the words of Jesus Christ.

What Does "Forever and Ever" Mean?

We could rest the case here and call it proven, but let us turn to another passage, Revelation 14:9–11:

*Then a third angel followed them, saying with
a loud voice, "If anyone worships the beast*

and his image, and receives his mark on his forehead or on his hand, he himself shall also drink of the wine of the wrath of God, which is poured out full strength into the cup of His indignation. He shall be tormented with fire and brimstone in the presence of the holy angels and in the presence of the Lamb. And the smoke of their torment ascends forever and ever; and they have no rest day or night, who worship the beast and his image, and whoever receives the mark of his name."

Here we have another expression for the duration of the suffering of the impenitent, the expression rendered *"forever and ever."* In the Greek, there are two slightly different forms of expression that are translated in this way. The one form of expression, rendered literally, is "unto the ages of the ages"; the other form is "unto ages of ages."

What thought do these expressions convey? Those who seek to escape the fact that these words refer to absolute endlessness say that the expressions are a Hebraism* for "the supreme one of its class." As illustrations of the same alleged Hebraism, they cite the names *Lord of Lords* and *Holy of Holies*.

But their theory is not true. In the first place, neither of these two names have the same form as "unto the ages of the ages." In the second place, the definition they give is not even the meaning of the names *Lord of Lords* and *Holy of Holies*. The expression *Lord of Lords* does not mean merely the

---

* A Hebraism is a feature that is characteristic of Hebrew and that occurs in another language.

greatest Lord, but One who is Himself Lord of all other lords. Likewise, this expression *unto the ages of the ages* never means merely the ages that are the supreme ages as distinct from other ages (nor, as someone else put it, "the ages that *come out of* the other ages," that is, the closing ages before eternity). The expression, according to its form, means ages that are themselves composed of ages. It represents not years tumbling upon years, nor centuries tumbling upon centuries, but ages tumbling upon ages in endless procession. It is the strongest possible form of expression for absolute endlessness.

Furthermore, the way to determine conclusively what *"forever and ever"* means is by considering its usage. Usage is always the decisive thing in determining the meaning of words and phrases. What is the usage of this expression in the book from which we have taken our passage? The expression *"forever and ever"* is used thirteen times in the book of Revelation. In nine of the thirteen times, it refers to the duration of the existence, reign, or glory of God and of His Son, Jesus Christ our Lord. Of course, in these instances, it must not represent merely the supreme ages, or any individual ages—it must refer to absolute eternity and endlessness. Once it is used of the duration of the blessed reign of the righteous, and, of course, here again it refers to an endless eternity. In the three remaining instances, it is used of the duration of the torment of the Devil, the Beast, the False Prophet, and the persistently impenitent.

Those who deny that *"forever and ever"* means an absolutely endless eternity use the following argument. They point out that the phrase is used in Revelation 11:15, where we are told *"the kingdoms* of this world have become the kingdoms of our Lord and of His Christ, and He shall reign forever and ever ["unto the ages of the ages"]!" They add that we are told in 1 Corinthians 15:24 that Christ *"delivers the kingdom to God the Father."* Therefore, His kingdom must come to an end, and consequently, *"forever and ever"* in this passage cannot mean without end.

There are two answers to this objection, either of which is sufficient. The first is that the *"He"* in *"He shall reign forever and ever"* does not necessarily refer to the Christ, but rather to the Lord Jehovah. In this case, their argument falls to the ground.

The second answer is that while we are taught in 1 Corinthians 15:24, and elsewhere, that Jesus Christ will deliver up His *mediatorial* kingdom to the Father, we are distinctly taught that He will rule with the Father. We are told in Luke 1:33 that *"of His kingdom there will be no end."* Therefore, even if the *"He"* in Revelation 11:15 refers to the Christ and not to the Lord Jehovah, the statement is exactly correct. He, the Christ, is to reign *"forever and ever,"* that is, without end.

There is not a single passage in the whole book of Revelation in which *"forever and ever"* is used of anything except what is absolutely endless. So the question is answered again, and answered decisively, that the conscious suffering of the persistently impenitent is absolutely endless.

What Does "Everlasting Destruction" Mean?

Now let us look at another passage, 2 Thessalonians 1:7–9:

The Lord Jesus [will be] *revealed from heaven with His mighty angels, in flaming fire taking vengeance on those who do not know God, and on those who do not obey the gospel of our Lord Jesus Christ. These shall be punished with everlasting destruction from the presence of the Lord and from the glory of His power.*

Here we are told that the punishment of those who *"do not know God"* and *"do not obey the gospel"* is *"everlasting destruction."*

What does *"everlasting destruction"* mean? In the previous chapter, "Is There a Literal Hell?" we saw that the biblical meaning of *"destruction"* is a portion in the lake of fire. We saw, moreover, that the inhabitants of the lake of fire *"will be tormented day and night forever and ever"* (Rev. 20:10). It is clear, then, that those who do not know God and do not obey the gospel of our Lord Jesus Christ will be punished with never ending, conscious suffering.

What Does "Everlasting Fire" Mean?

Let us look at one more passage, Matthew 25:41, where Jesus said,

Then He [the Lord Jesus Himself] *will also say to those on the left hand, "Depart from Me, you cursed, into the everlasting fire prepared for the devil and his angels."*

What I want you to notice here is that the punishment into which the impenitent are sent is the *"everlasting fire"* that is *"prepared for the devil and his angels."* In Revelation 20:10, we have an exact description of just what the eternal fire prepared for the Devil and his angels is:

> *The devil, who deceived them, was cast into the lake of fire and brimstone where the beast and the false prophet are. And they will be tormented day and night forever and ever.*

By a comparison of these two statements, we have another explicit declaration of our Lord that the punishment of the impenitent is to be a conscious agony. They will be punished *"day and night"* without rest *"forever and ever."*

From any one of these passages, and especially from all of them put together, we see that the Scriptures make it as plain as language can make it that the future punishment of the persistently impenitent will be absolutely endless.

Arguments against the Endlessness of Future Punishment

Those who believe that all people will ultimately repent, accept Christ, and be saved urge several Scriptures against what seems to be the plain teaching of the passages we have been studying.

Christ Preached to the Spirits in Prison

The first of these is 1 Peter 3:18–20:

> *For Christ also suffered once for sins, the just for the unjust, that He might bring us to God,*

> *being put to death in the flesh but made alive*
> *by the Spirit, by whom also He went and*
> *preached to the spirits in prison, who formerly*
> *were disobedient, when once the Divine long-*
> *suffering waited in the days of Noah, while the*
> *ark was being prepared, in which a few, that*
> *is, eight souls, were saved through water.*

It is urged that since Christ went and preached to
the spirits in prison, there will be another chance for
people to be saved after they have died. But the passage in question does not assert or imply this idea in
any way.

First of all, there is no proof that *"the spirits in
prison"* refers to the departed spirits of people who
once lived here on earth. In the Bible, departed
spirits of people are not spoken of in this way. These
words are used of other spirits, but not of disembodied human spirits. There is every reason for sup-
posing that these *"spirits in prison"* were not the
sinful people who were on the earth when the ark
was being prepared, but the angels referred to in
Genesis 6:1–2 who sinned at that time. (See also
Jude 6–7.)

Furthermore, even if *"the spirits in prison"* here
spoken of were the spirits of people who were disobedient in the time of Noah, there is not a hint in
the passage that they were saved through the
preaching of Christ to them, or that they had another chance. There are two words commonly used
in the New Testament for preaching. One is *kerusso,*
and the other is *euaggelizo.* The first of these means
"to herald," as in heralding a king, or heralding a
kingdom. It may, however, be used of preaching a

message—the gospel message or some other message. The second word, *euaggelizo,* means "to preach the Gospel." In the passage that we are studying, the word *kerusso* is used, and there is not a hint that Christ preached the Gospel to these spirits in prison. His message was not a saving message; He simply heralded the triumph of the kingdom. So there is nothing in this passage that contradicts the plain, direct statements regarding the destiny of the wicked found in the passages we have been studying.

Those "under the earth" Will Bow to Christ

The second passage that is appealed to by those who deny the endlessness of future punishment is Philippians 2:9–11:

> *Therefore God also has highly exalted Him and given Him the name which is above every name, that at the name of Jesus every knee should bow, of those in heaven, and of those on earth, and of those under the earth, and that every tongue should confess that Jesus Christ is Lord, to the glory of God the Father.*

Here it is said that all those *"under the earth,"* as well as all those in heaven and on earth, will bow the knee at the name of Jesus and confess that Jesus Christ is Lord. Some people say that this verse implies that all those *"under the earth"* will be saved. But it does not imply this idea at all. Every knee of every lost individual—and of the Devil and of his angels, too—will be forced someday to bow at the name of Jesus, and every tongue will be forced to confess that He is Lord. If anyone does that in the present life of his own free choice, he will be saved; otherwise, he will do it by compulsion in the age to come. Everyone has to choose between doing it now willingly and gladly, and being saved, or doing it in the hereafter by compulsion, and being lost. There is absolutely nothing in this passage that teaches universal salvation or that even implies anything that weakens the plain statements we have been studying.

All Things Will Be Restored

The third passage that is appealed to is Acts 3:19–21:

> *Repent therefore and be converted, that your sins may be blotted out, so that times of refreshing may come from the presence of the Lord, and that He may send Jesus Christ, who was preached to you before, whom heaven must receive until the times of restoration of all things, which God has spoken by the mouth of all His holy prophets since the world began.*

Here we are told of a coming *"restoration of all things."* Those who contend for the doctrine of universal salvation believe that this means the restoration to righteousness of all persons. But that is not what this passage says, and that is not what it refers to.

We are taught in Old Testament prophecy, and also in the book of Romans, that in connection with the return of our Lord Jesus, there is going to be a restoration of all nature—of the whole physical universe—from its fallen state. For example, in Romans 8:19–21, we read,

> *For the earnest expectation of the creation eagerly waits for the revealing of the sons of God. For the creation was subjected to futility, not willingly, but because of Him who subjected it in hope; because the creation itself also will be delivered from the bondage of corruption into the glorious liberty of the children of God.*

In Isaiah 55:13, we read,

> *Instead of the thorn shall come up the cypress tree, and instead of the brier shall come up the myrtle tree; and it shall be to the LORD for a name, for an everlasting sign that shall not be cut off.*

In Isaiah 65:25, we are told,

> *"The wolf and the lamb shall feed together, the lion shall eat straw like the ox, and dust shall be the serpent's food. They shall not hurt nor destroy in all My holy mountain," says the LORD.*

And in Isaiah 32:15, we read,

> *The Spirit is poured upon us from on high, and the wilderness becomes a fruitful field, and the fruitful field is counted as a forest.*

It is to this restoration of the physical universe, plainly predicted here in Romans 8:19–21 and these

Old Testament prophecies, that the *"restoration of all things"* spoken of in Acts 3:21 refers. There is not a hint, not the slightest suggestion, of a restoration of impenitent sinners.

All Things in Heaven and on Earth Will Be Summed Up in Christ

Still another passage that is urged is Ephesians 1:9–10, where we read,

[God] *made known to us the mystery of His will, according to His good pleasure which He purposed in Himself, that in the dispensation of the fullness of the times He might gather together in one all things in Christ, both which are in heaven and which are on earth; in Him.*

Here it is urged that things in heaven and things on earth are to be summed up in Christ. This is true, but it should be noticed that the Holy Spirit has specifically omitted here the phrase that is found in Philippians 2:10, *"those under the earth,"* that is, the abode of the lost. So this passage, far from suggesting that the lost ones in hell will be restored, suggests exactly the opposite. There is, then, certainly nothing in this passage to contradict the plain doctrine of the eternal punishment of the unsaved.

All Will Be Made Alive in Christ

One more passage that is urged against the truth we have been studying remains to be considered: 1 Corinthians 15:22. Here we read, *"For as in*

Adam all die, even so in Christ all shall be made alive." Some say that we are distinctly told here that all who die in Adam, that is, every human being, will be made alive in Christ, and that *"made alive"* means "to obtain eternal life" or "to be saved."

For years I thought that this was the true interpretation of this passage. For this reason, in part, I believed and preached that all people ultimately—sometime, somewhere, somehow—would be brought to accept Jesus Christ and be saved. But when I came to study this verse more carefully, I saw that this was a misinterpretation of the passage.

Every passage in the Bible, or in any other book, must be interpreted in its context. The whole subject that Paul was talking about in this chapter is not the immortality of the soul, but *the resurrection of the body*. All this passage declares is that, just as all lose physical life in Adam, so also all will obtain a resurrection of the body in Christ. Whether that resurrection of the body is a resurrection to *"everlasting life"* or a resurrection to *"shame and everlasting contempt"* (Dan. 12:2) depends entirely on what people do with Jesus Christ. Absolutely nothing in 1 Corinthians 15:22 teaches universal salvation. It only teaches a universal resurrection—a resurrection of the wicked as well as a resurrection of the righteous.

So these are the passages that are so often urged to prove universal salvation. We have seen that there is nothing in any one of them, or in all of them put together, to teach that all people will ultimately be saved. Furthermore, nothing in them conflicts with what we have seen to be the honest meaning of the passages studied earlier in this chapter, namely, that the future punishment of sin is absolutely endless.

Not one passage in the Bible teaches that all people will ultimately come to repentance and be saved. I wish that there were one, but there is not. Though I have been searching diligently for such a passage for nearly forty years, I have not found it, and it cannot be found.

Is There a Chance to Be Saved after Death?

One other important question remains: Where are the issues of eternity settled? Some who believe that the punishment of the persistently impenitent is everlasting, that it has no end, nevertheless believe that the issues of eternity are not settled in this present life. They believe that many people settle these issues after death, and that when people die impenitent, they will have another chance. So we see that if someone believes in endless punishment, he does not necessarily believe that there is no chance to be saved after death. Many believe that there will be a chance after death, that many will accept it, and that some will not accept it and will therefore be punished forever and ever.

Now, what is the teaching of the Word of God on this point? Let me call your attention to four passages, any one of which settles the question. Taken together, they leave no possible room for doubt for any honest person who is willing to take the Bible as meaning what it says and who is not merely trying to support a theory.

The first passage is 2 Corinthians 5:10:

For we must all appear before the judgment seat of Christ, that each one may receive the

*things done in the body, according to what he
has done, whether good or bad.*

In this passage, we are plainly told that the basis of
judgment in the world to come is *"the things done in
the body,"* that is, the things done before the spirit
leaves the body, the things done before we exit this
world. Of course, this particular passage has to do
primarily with the judgment of the believer, but it
shows what the basis of future judgment is, namely,
the things done this side of the grave.

The second passage is Hebrews 9:27: *"It is ap-
pointed for men to die once, but after this the judgment."* Here we are distinctly told that after death
there is to be, not an opportunity to prepare for
judgment, but judgment itself, and that therefore
our destiny is settled *at death.* There is no chance of
salvation after death.

The third passage is John 5:28–29:

*Do not marvel at this; for the hour is coming
in which all who are in the graves will hear
His voice and come forth; those who have done
good, to the resurrection of life, and those who
have done evil, to the resurrection of condemnation.*

Here, also, it is clearly implied that the resurrection
of the good and the bad is for the purpose of judgment regarding the things they did before their
bodies were laid in the grave.

A fourth passage—and, if possible, a more decisive passage than any of these—is John 8:21: *"Then
Jesus said to them* [the Pharisees] *again, 'I am going*

away, and you will seek Me, and will die in your sin. Where I go you cannot come.'" Here our Lord distinctly declared that the question of whether people will go to be with Him or not depends on what they do *before* they die. If they die in their sins, they will not go to be with Him.

We see from these passages that the issues of eternity—the issues of eternal blessedness and glory or eternal agony and shame—are settled in the life that now is.

Do You Believe in Eternal Punishment?

The future state of those who, in this life, reject the redemption offered to them in Christ Jesus is a state of conscious, unutterable, endless torment and anguish. This concept is appalling, but it is scriptural. It is the unmistakable, inescapable teaching of God's own Word.

I wish that all people would repent and accept Christ. If anyone could show me one single passage in the Bible that clearly teaches that every individual will ultimately repent, accept Christ, and be saved, it would be the happiest day of my life, but it cannot be found. I once thought it could, and I believed and taught according to this line of reasoning. These ideas that are so widely circulated today—these theories of Charles Taze Russell and many others—are not at all new to me. I held and taught substantially the same views regarding ultimate universal salvation nearly forty years ago. I was familiar with the arguments that others now urge, and other more persuasive arguments that they do not seem to know.

But the time came, as I studied the Bible more carefully, when I could not reconcile my teaching with what I found to be the unmistakable teaching of God's Word. I had three choices: to give up my belief that the Bible is the Word of God, to twist the words of Jesus (and others in the New Testament) to mean something other than what they clearly teach, or to give up my doctrine of ultimate universal restoration and salvation.

I could not give up my belief that the Bible is the Word of God, for I had found absolutely overwhelming proof that it is God's Word. I could not twist the words of Jesus and of others to mean something other than their clearly intended meaning, for I was an honest man. There was only one thing left to do, and that was to give up my doctrine of universal restoration and salvation. I gave it up with great reluctance, but I was compelled to give it up or to be untrue to my own reason and conscience. It is the inescapable teaching of the Word of God that all who leave this world without having accepted Jesus Christ will spend eternity in hell—a hell of unutterable, conscious anguish.

This biblical concept is a reasonable one when we come to see the appalling nature of sin, and especially the sin of trampling underfoot God's mercy toward sinners and rejecting God's glorious Son, whom in His love He has provided as a Savior. (See Hebrews 10:29.)

Shallow views of sin, God's holiness, and the glory of Jesus Christ lie at the bottom of weak theories of the doom of the impenitent. When we see sin in all its hideousness and enormity, the holiness of God in all its perfection, and the glory of Jesus

Christ in all its infinity, nothing will satisfy the demands of our own moral intuitions but the doctrine of the endless, conscious suffering of the lost. Those who persist in the choice of sin, who love darkness rather than light (John 3:19), and who persist in the rejection of the Son of God, will endure everlasting anguish. Nothing but the fact that we dread suffering more than we loathe sin, that we avoid sorrow more than we love the glory of Jesus Christ, makes us reject the thought that beings who eternally choose sin should eternally suffer.

In spite of people's sin, God offers them mercy in this life. In fact, He made the tremendous sacrifice of His Son to save them. However, many despise that mercy and trample God's Son underfoot (Heb. 10:29). If, then, they are consigned to everlasting torment, I cannot help but say, "Amen! Hallelujah! *'True and righteous are Your judgments'* (Rev. 16:7)!"

At any rate, the doctrine of conscious, eternal torment for impenitent individuals is clearly revealed in the Word of God. Whether we can defend it on philosophical grounds or not, it is our business to believe it and to leave it to the clearer light of eternity to explain what we cannot now understand. We must realize that God may have many infinitely wise reasons for doing things for which we, in our ignorance, can see no sufficient reason at all. It is the most ludicrous pride for beings so limited and foolish as the wisest of men are, to attempt to dogmatize how a God of infinite wisdom must act. All we know about how God is to act is what God has seen fit to tell us.

In conclusion, two things are certain. First, the more closely people walk with God and the more devoted they become in His service, the more likely they are to believe this doctrine. Many people say that they love their fellowmen too much to believe it. But the people who show their love in more practical ways than by sentimental protests about this doctrine, the people who show their love for their fellowmen as Jesus Christ showed His, by laying down their lives for them—these people believe this doctrine, even as Jesus Christ Himself believed it.

As Christians become worldly and lazy, they grow loose in their doctrine concerning the doom of the impenitent. The fact that loose doctrines are spreading so rapidly and widely in our day, and that worldliness is also spreading in the church, testifies against them. (See 1 Timothy 4:1–2; 2 Timothy 3:1–5; 4:2–4.) Increasing laxity of life and increasing laxity of doctrine go hand in hand.

The second thing that is certain is that people who accept a loose doctrine regarding the ultimate penalty of sin lose their power for God. I have seen this fact proven over and over again. These people are very clever at argument and are very zealous in proselytizing, but they are seldom found pleading with others to be reconciled to God (2 Cor. 5:20). They are far more likely to be found trying to upset the faith of people already won by the efforts of those who do believe in everlasting punishment than trying to win people who have no faith at all.

If you really believe the doctrine of the endless torment of the impenitent, if the doctrine really gets hold of you, you will work as you have never worked before for the salvation of the lost. Lessening the doctrine in any way will lessen your zeal. Time and time again, I have come to this awful doctrine and tried to find some way of escape from it. But when I have failed—as I have always done at last when I have determined to be honest with the Bible and myself—I have returned to my work with an increased burden for souls and an intensified determination to *"spend and be spent"* for their salvation (2 Cor. 12:15).

Eternal, conscious suffering—suffering without the least hope of relief—awaits every one of you reading this who goes on persistently rejecting Jesus Christ and who passes out of this world having rejected Him. In that world of never ending gloom, there will be no possibility of repentance. As you look out into the future, there will not be one single ray of hope. *"Forever and ever"* will be the unceasing wail of that restless sea of fire. After you have been there ten million years and look out toward the future, you will see eternity still stretching on and on and on, with no hope.

Oh, men and women outside of Christ, why will you risk such a doom for a single year, or a month, or a week, or a day? Hell is too awful to risk for five minutes the chance of going there. There is but one rational thing for you to do, and that is to accept Christ right now as your Savior, surrender to Him as your Lord and Master, confess Him as such before the world, and strive from this time on to please Him in everything, day by day. Any other choice is absolute madness.